Jahanzaib Imtiaz

Route Transmission & Control Applications and Java Web Services

Jahanzaib Imtiaz

Route Transmission & Control Applications and Java Web Services

Route Transmission and Control Using a Java EE5 Web Service and a Vehicle Based Mobile Device (Cellular phone or a PDA with GPS)

VDM Verlag Dr. Müller

Imprint

Bibliographic information by the German National Library: The German National Library lists this publication at the German National Bibliography; detailed bibliographic information is available on the Internet at http://dnb.d-nb.de.

Cover image: www.purestockx.com

Publisher:
VDM Verlag Dr. Müller Aktiengesellschaft & Co. KG , Dudweiler Landstr. 125 a, 66123 Saarbrücken, Germany,
Phone +49 681 9100-698, Fax +49 681 9100-988,
Email: info@vdm-verlag.de

Zugl.: Lemgo, FH, Diss, 2007

Produced in USA and UK by:
Lightning Source Inc., La Vergne, Tennessee, USA
Lightning Source UK Ltd., Milton Keynes, UK
BookSurge LLC, 5341 Dorchester Road, Suite 16, North Charleston, SC 29418, USA

ISBN: 978-3-8364-7506-8

Acknowledgments

The author would like to thank the myriad persons who provided support and encouragement throughout the pursuit of this study work. In particular:

Prof. Dr.-Ing. Thomas Korte, for given me the motivation to work on the subject and guided through in right direction. Very special thanks are due to Dipl.-Ing. Sönke Hoffmann for his advice and guidance when I felt stuck in progress. Thanks to Mr. Ahmad Ali Tabassam and Mr. Li Rui for their time to review the study report, and to my fellow colleagues during master studies for their moral support and general helping hand.

Special thanks to my parents and sisters, who provided the item of greatest worth - opportunity. Thank you for standing by me through the many trials and decisions of my educational career.

Table of Contents

Abbreviations

LTCS	Location Tracking & Control System
GPS	Global Positioning System
PDA	Personal Data Advisor
SOAP	Simple Object Access Protocol
GPRS	General Packet Radio Service
XML	Extensible Markup Language
UML	Unified Modeling Language
MS	Mobile Subscriber
SMS	Short Message Service
GSM	Global System for Mobile Communications
ITS	Intelligent Transportation Systems
NEMA	National Electrical Manufacturers Association
SIM	Subscriber Identity Module
ICS	Internet Connection Service
WAP	Wireless Application Protocol
WLAN	Wireless Local Area Network
API	Application Program Interface
CLDC	Connected Limited Device Configuration
GUI	Graphical User Interface
HTTP	Hypertext Transfer Protocol
TCP/IP	Transmission Control Protocol / Internet Protocol
UTC	Coordinated Universal Time
PNG	Portable Network Graphics
RFCOMM	Radio Frequency Communication
JSP	Java Server pages
URL	Uniform Resource Locator
SOA	Service Oriented Architecture

| WSDL | Web Services Description Language |
| J2ME | Java 2 Micro Edition |

List of Figures

List of Tables

1   Introduction

This section discusses the author's motivation and objectives to the subject, and gives a brief overview of different chapters of the study report.

1.1   Motivation

Knowledge about exact geographical location of certain target objects are always a point of interest in many business applications. Associating timestamp to such information makes it more valuable. This enables applications to track target objects (Vehicles for example) in certain period.

By keeping a record of live & continuous positional information of mobile assets, many organizations could be able to manage, optimize, and control their mobile resource.

There are many applications [7-18, 35-42], and many more would be possible if there could be some technologies that enables such applications to communicate with each other. Here comes the idea of interoperability, to provide wide range of services to the diverse classes of consumers.

An interesting scenario is, imagine a manger monitoring employees working in field area, during a lunch time he wants to know about a pizza delivery van nearby, monitor's company transport fleet and directing individual vehicles for next job, also worried for whereabouts of his family and wants to watch if kids are at school or making day out. Doing this all from a computer at his office, or while roaming around with a PDA in his pocket.

This study work is an effort to address such applications and their interoperability. The idea is driven by a foundation *Eben-Ezer* in Lemgo, a diaconal institution for people with mental disabilities. They require a simple solution to remotely control and manage their transport system with relatively small number of vehicles. Aim of the project is to develop a model application for proof of concept.

The idea is to use a Global Position System for location identification, and cost efficiently use General Packet Radio Service technology for communication of data between mobile units and track servers. There is already lot of work has done in Location Tracking & Control Systems using GPS technologies [1-5]. This study mainly focus on finding, how far Simple Object Access Protocol based Web Services could be integrated into the LTCS to track [55], control and monitor mobile units, and to transmit directional routes to them.

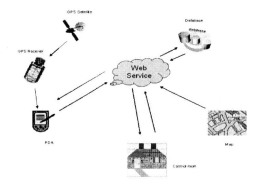

Figure 1: Theoretical framework.

1.2   Significance of the Work

This study work addresses the three major problems.

- Is it possible to have a program that reside into mobile device (PDA), that could collect information from a Bluetooth enabled GPS device and can transmit the processed information to a server via a Web Service using SOAP messages?

- Is it possible to have a Web Service that could get positional information from the mobile devices, implements all business logic, and stores it into a database and presents information to the supervisor application when requested?

- Is it possible to have a monitoring application that can provide a support to the supervisor, to visualize current location of mobile objects, able to trace movement history, allow sending messages, and directional routes, through Web Service?

This study can be a significant contribution to the modern practices for controlling the rescue activities, transport management, commercial applications, surveillance, security, and military operations.

1.3   Background to the Study

The recent popularity and adoption of the Internet and Web Services has provided a new means of interoperability for geospatial information, differing from previous approaches to information exchange [55].

Web Services are business services that allow "dynamic (run-time) application-to-application integration. They can be used for business-to-business integration and/or for Enterprise Application Integration within companies" [2]. The extensibility and flexibility of Web Services as a client server model, could be an ideal solution for LTCS. This is the reason why author proposed them for *Eben-Ezer* in this study work.

Satellite navigation receivers are now commonly installed in new cars as a key tool for providing new services, to the peoples moving around. Real-time traffic information, emergency calls, route guidance, fleet management and Advanced Driving Assistance Systems (ADAS) [3] are some key application areas. There are already some solutions available in the market by different vender's for example SMARTFLEET Manager [1], Global Tracking Communications Inc [4], ThinkGeo [5]. Because of positional accuracy GPS becomes an ideal choice for proposed LTCS. Subsequent chapters gives more technical details about the subject and describes how the system is realized. Following paragraphs gives a short introduction for each chapter.

Chapter 2, *Technologies & Background* provides a reader sufficient background about available technologies, possible data communication & software development techniques, their advantages and disadvantages on each other (Cost factors). This section also includes a matrix of technical details, that allows perceiving the advantages and disadvantages of the proposed approach with already in market approaches.

Chapter 3, *Web Service Security* discusses how to secure Web Services and what kind of special location related standards should be consider while implementing the security.

Chapter 4, *Model Application for proof of Concept* demonstrates the architectural view of the proposed application and provides a detail design aspect. A UML based object oriented approach has been used to model the different components of the proposed system.

Chapter 5, *System Test Cases* shows some vital application flows tested to insure that physical application meets the design goals. Due to the R&D orientation of the project Spiral Model [6] has been used during software development process.

Chapter 6, *Conclusion and Future Work* discusses the achievements of the project work, problems encountered during the course of study and purposes the possible future extensions in the subject area.

A list of possible error messages and a complete guide about the setup of application development and deployment environment can be seen in appendixes.

2   Technologies & Background

2.1   Overview

This chapter discusses the current technologies that contribute into the location tracking & control applications, intension of the author is to develop an understanding for the reader about the topic, and provide them sufficient background about the context, specific to study topic.

This chapter starts by discussing the domain where location based application fall in, also defining the related technologies, possible cost effective strategies, required development environment for tracking & control applications, necessary equipment, cost factor of different possibilities. It also provides an overview of the existing applications and methodologies adopted into different application areas, and how proposed one makes difference? and possible pros and cons for both cases.

2.2   Web Based Location Services

One purpose of the study document is to provide guidance on how to architect end-to-end location services in a SOAP based Web Service environment. SOAP is a protocol for exchanging XML-based messages on computer networks, normally using HTTP/HTTPS, in which one network node (the *client*) sends a request message, to another node (the *server*) and the server immediately sends a response message to the client [7].

Location services are classified into three different classes. Each class includes a set of services which shares the same requirements and has the same functionality [7].

Table 1: Location service classification [7].

Class 1: Self positioning	Class 2: Tracking	Class 3:Registration
• Road assistance • Health monitoring • Rescue service • Closest attraction	Tracking on demand • Asset tracking • Child locator • Stolen vehicles locator	• Weather alerts • Location specific advertising • location based WAP push

• Personal/vehicle navigator
• Locate attractions along the route
	Continuous tracking
	• Fleet management
	• Vehicle tracking
	• Automatic tracking and alert
	• Turn by turn directions
		• "Geofit" applications:
		   o prisoner inside restricted area
		   o fixed asset moved

2.2.1 Class 1: Positioning or Self Location Search: "Here I am"

A mobile subscriber (MS) locates itself first and requests the content server to send him information that relates to his position. During the location phase, the mobile subscriber may have its own position locally available or may ask the network for assistance .

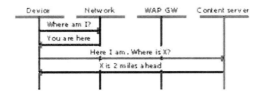

2.2.2 Class 2: Tracking On Demand and Continuous Tracking

Two use cases should be considered for this class:

Tracking on demand: "Where is he?"

An authorized application tracks the MS. The location request goes to the MS. The MS determines its location by whatever means is supported and reports this information back to the requestor [7].

Continuous tracking: "Where is he? ...Where is he? ...Where is he?"

This is the main interesting class for study work; here content server (GPSTrackServer) requests the mobile device to return its position continuously. The time interval between consecutive location updates, may be specified by the server [7].

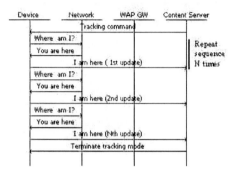

2.2.3 Class 3: Registration or Self Location Report: *"He is here"*

The mobile subscriber receives pushed information based on the area where it is located. Typically the area is predefined by the Internet application. For example, it may be desirable to push the advertisements to the devices that are inside the shopping mall [7].

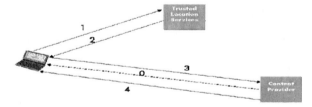

2.2.4 Where Does the Location Information Reside?

Going back to the previous section, it is clear that for a given class of service, the message flow chart depends on who owns the location information and who asks for it [7].

It is anticipated that the location information will reside either at the mobile station (example: autonomous GPS technology) which is the case in this study work, or at the wireless network side (example: O2, T-Mobile).

2.3   Tracking & Control

As the study work is about controlling and monitoring the vehicles for *Eben-Ezer*, so before going further, it will be a good to discuss some basics of vehicle tracking & control and how they have been applied in this study work.

A vehicle tracking is a way of monitoring the location, movements, status and behavior of a vehicle or fleet of vehicles. This is achieved through a combination of a GPS receiver and an electronic device (usually comprising a GSM GPRS modem or SMS sender) installed in each vehicle, communicating with the user (dispatching, emergency or coordinating unit) and PC or web-based software. The data are turned into information by management reporting tools in conjunction with a visual display on computerized Mapping software [6].

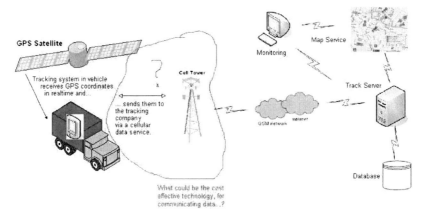

Figure 2 Tracking & Control Basics

A point of interest with respect to this study work, with in this communication structure is to use cost effective technology, for communication of dataflow from mobile unit to the track server, we will discuss about possible options later in this chapter.

There are certain standards including Intelligent Transportation Systems (ITS) Standards [20]-[22]], IEEE Vehicular Technology Society [23], and NEMA. It is recommended to follow these standards to ensure the interoperability among such applications. This project utilizes $GPGGA format string of NEMA standard for parsing and extracting positional information from data read from GPS, and also some guidelines from ITS. A brief overview of these standards is given below.

2.3.1 Intelligent Transportation Systems (ITS) Standards

ITS improves transportation safety, mobility and enhance the productivity through a use of advanced communications technologies [20]-[22].

Intelligent transportation systems (ITS) encompass a broad range of wireless and wired communications-based information and electronics technologies. ITS standards are industry-consensus standards that define how system components operate within a consistent framework. This framework is known as the National ITS Architecture which specifying how different systems and components interconnects to promote interoperability [22].

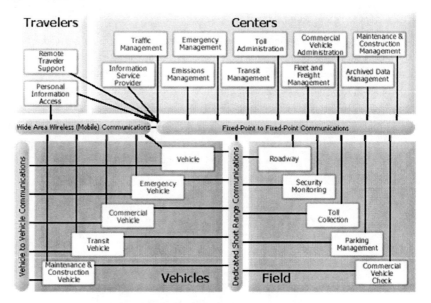

Figure 3: (ITS) Architecture [20].

2.3.2 NEMA

The National Marine Electronics Association (NMEA) has developed a specification that defines the GPS receiver's communication data format [24].

This project work uses a GGA sentence of NEMA, because it provides the essential fix data, and also the possible error status, which could be used to discard erroneous sentence and to use the next coming one. See Appendix D for detail about GGA string.

2.3.3 Location Identification Technologies

It will be interesting to know that what are different possible location identification technologies and how they works, some times these technologies used in conjunction to each other based on the specific application needs (accuracy, latency, response time etc). They normally fall into three categories.

2.3.4 GSM Cell Based Tracking & Control

Many application [8][10] are using cellular networks (GSM or others) to calculate the position of target objects. There are three different geo positioning techniques, cell identification, time difference and triangulation [11].

In these techniques the location of a mobile unit is identified using the existing infrastructure of service provider, by collecting information of the current cell and surrounding cells, then making calculations (triangulation commonly) based on that information. Normally the calculated location is accurate up to a few hundred meters in cities, and up to a few kilometers in countryside [11].

The cellular network based tracking is an inexpensive technology but we got to compromise on the accuracy of the location, in tracking system for Eben-Ezer, we need more precise location for the target mobile unit in order to know its track within the urban region.

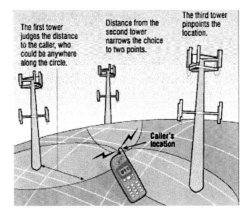

Figure 4: Cell based location identification.

2.3.5 Radio Frequency (RF) Tracking

These systems [15] are very expensive, complex and only used for military or security applications, they also require extra and dedicated hardware and infrastructure to realize the operations. This study work is not directly related to such systems, like VectorTrac [13] and LoJack [14]. More details about RF tracking could be found in [12].

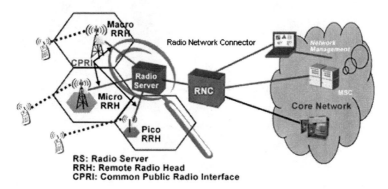

RS: Radio Server
RRH: Remote Radio Head
CPRI: Common Public Radio Interface

Figure 5: RF Location identification [16].

2.3.6 Global Positioning System (GPS) Tracking

Open air tracking & control involves at the earth positional information, so far the only source exist in space is U.S based GPS, other alternative is still has to come as Galileo positioning system by EU. This project uses the pure GPS technologies to correctly identify the position of target object in terms of latitude and longitude [6],[17].

The current GPS consists of three major segments. A space segment (SS) composed of the GPS satellites that transmits time and position to the user segment. The space segment has an arrangement of 24 satellites that is called a "constellation". A control segment (CS) that monitors and controls the satellites. A user segment (US), a specialized radio receiver designed to listen to the radio signals being transmitted from the satellites and calculate the position by applying the trilateration methods on the received information [6],[49][52]. This project uses GPS mouse as user segment for this purpose (See Appendix B).

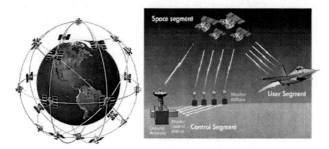

Figure 6: GPS technologies [51]-[52].

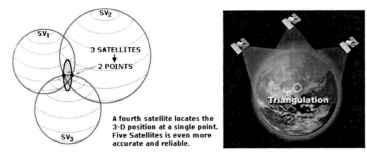

Figure 7: GPS position calculation (Trilateration) [50]-[51].

A GPS receiver receives radio signals, from 24 satellites orbiting around the earth. If a receiver receive the signals from at least 3 satellites, simultaneously, then it can calculate its own location, usually accurate to within a few feet. At this point, these location information must somehow be transmitted to a base station to be displayed on a computerized Map. This can be accomplished in a number of ways each with its own set of unique advantages and disadvantages [12], [18]. Most common, is to send the data over an analog cellular phone data channel or GSM GPRS [18]. Another option is to send the data over a dialup cellular connection, or data can be sent as a Short Message Service (SMS) message. Yet another option would be to send the data over a satellite communication link, or lastly, over a local analog or digital radio system [12]. Each method has its own pros & cons and associated cost factor. We will discuss some of them in little more detail at subsequent section.

2.4   Data Communication, Protocols & Strategies

At the same time, the GPS tracking device (combination of mobile phone and GPS mouse) is determining its position, it also tries to establish a connection to a cellular communication network. By using a SIM (the small card that goes into the mobile phone) it connects over the air to the nearest cell tower. This is the same technology used for making calls, except in this case, we are transmitting data instead of a voice conversation. During a data connection, the cellular provider allows the device to access the internet, using the setup information programmed into the device (See Appendix C). The device then attempts to connect to the internet address defined by mobile worker as the access server. Contacting the server, the mobile device sends its unique identifier to the server, and a live communication link will be established between mobile device and the server. Location information such as the vehicle's current position will be sent using the established connection. In the event that the connection is broken, the GPS Transmitter application residing on phone will repeat these steps automatically to assure a new connection [19].

GPS tracking device is a combination of a GPS receiver and a GSM modem. There are many possibilities in order to realize such devices, which are purely based on the application requirements. In our model application Author has used the separate Bluetooth enabled GPS mouse (Holux GPSlim236), Mobile phones (Nokia E65, Nokia 8260, and Sony Ericsson 990i), and a software application residing on mobile phone to realize the communication.

Figure 8: Mobile equipment used for project.

2.4.1 Communication Protocols

There could be many protocols to realize such data communication. For this study work Author has used GPRS/ICS (Internet Communications Services) of a GSM based cellular network; following cite that how *Wikipedia (an online encyclopedia)* describes some possible protocols, each of them has a certain advantages and disadvantages.

- *Short Message Service (SMS):-* Often called text messaging, is a means of sending short messages to and from mobile phones. Normally sends messages of up to 160 characters, to and from GSM mobile handsets. Most SMS messages are mobile-to-mobile text messages, though the standard supports other types of broadcast messaging as well [6].

- *WAP Push:-* Allows WAP content to be pushed to the mobile handset with minimum user intervention. A WAP Push is basically a specially encoded message which includes a link to a WAP address. WAP Push messages have to be delivered on top of the SMS bearer. On receiving a WAP Push, a WAP 1.2 or later enabled handset will automatically give the user the option to access the WAP content. This is also known as WAP Push SI (Service Indication). The network entity that processes WAP Pushes and delivers them over an IP or SMS Bearer is known as a Push Proxy Gateway [6].

- *General Packet Radio Service (GPRS):-* A Mobile Data Service available to users of GSM mobile phones. GPRS data transfer is typically charged per megabyte of transferred data, while data communication via traditional circuit switching is billed per minute of connection time, independent of whether the user has actually transferred data or has been in an idle state [6].

SMS is charged on per message (packet) basis. In other words, it would cost same to send one or up to 160 characters since both would fit in one packet or message.

ICS is charged on a data (characters) transfer basis. For example, in Germany an SMS message could cost as 0.19 cent per (O2) message and ICS messages are charged as cheap as 0.01 cents for 1024 characters, then if 160 characters were sent by SMS, it would cost 0.19 cent. However if a message of 160 characters were sent via ICS, it would cost 0.0016 cent. The most dramatic difference in prices will occur if only 1 character was sent. It would cost 0.19 cent via SMS and 0.00001 cents via ICS [25].

Therefore sending messages via SMS is much more expensive then sending it via GPRS/ICS.

Table 2: Summarizes the differences between SMS and GPRS/ICS [25].

	SMS	**GPRS/ICS**
1.	Can only send text messages.	Can send any sort of messages that includes text, pictures and sound.
2.	Each message is limited up to 160 characters	There is no limit to the amount of data that can be sent.
3.	Messages are sent and delivered in packets.	Messages are streamed, like water in a water pipe.
4.	There is a delay between sending and receiving. This delay can be 15 seconds to several hours depending on congestion.	Data is received almost immediately when it is sent.
5.	Charges are based on per packet basis	Charges are based on a per character basis

Implications of Using GPRS/ICS in This System

As explained earlier, GPRS/ICS is neither as restrictive nor as costly as SMS. As such, much more can be done since a virtual direct circuit is present between the vehicle and the track server. It's data transmission is also much faster than SMS. This project based on GPRS/ICS so it can send more data and quickly, which helped to maintain the history of the journey and have far more reduced probability of "losing" a vehicle [25].

Request/Response strategy of SMS is engineered to send as little data as possible to reduce the data communications bills. The fewer requests for location are sent, the cheaper the bill would be but the consequence is that there is not much information in the form of history to process.

In our system, much more data is sent and the reason for doing so is functionality driven. Cost takes a second place because it is already priced very much cheap than SMS. The flexibility of GPRS/ICS begs to be exploited to achieve the objectives of the fleet managers. It will not be a surprise that the data communications bills will costs justifiably more than a SMS based LTCS [25].

Ultimately, the choice of price versus functionality is the prerogative of the fleet manager.

2.4.2 Communication Strategies & Impact of Cost

There could be many possible strategies based on one or more protocols as Author has discussed above, depending on the nature & volume of application and specific requirements in certain area, many tracking applications [4], [35]-[38], [43] use the SMS for data communication, some of them use WAP Push to communicate alerts and Maps [5], [38] other uses GPRS for data communication [41][42]. One idea was for this study work to promote SOAP based Web Services for location related applications, in order to realize such Web Services there will be a need of a constant data communication, regardless of data size. The GPRS/ICS is widely used protocol to achieve such architecture with the cellular networks [25].

Some application also uses hybrid communication scheme to fulfill their business domain requirements [39], for instance they uses GPRS technology to receive position base data at track server, and uses SMS to send supervisor alerts or messages [4], [35], also WAP Push to send Maps or run time application update patches, some uses email in certain cases as an alternative [39].

Of course each protocol comes with associated cost, our objective with this study work is to realize the most cost efficient architecture, cost efficient means the one that supports minimum data communication to exchange the maximum information.

SMS and WAP Push are complex in nature, requires installation of extra hardware, infrastructure and maintenance, that directly boost the cost. The SMS is also expensive and in our tracking system where there is a frequent location update after each 20 seconds (In urban area we need minimum update interval for sharp tracking performance) volume of sending SMS would be very high. SMS messages take time to deliver, and it's also expensive to send equal data as compared with GPRS technologies [25],[26]. Where as GPRS uses existing infrastructure, and cost comes only for the amount of data transferred. The developed model application is equally deployable on the alternative communication mediums like WLAN (in WiFi enabled cities).

A minimum data communication to exchange maximum information based on a logical flow of application, that's how the business flow is architected. Also depends on the development technology and its capabilities to minimize unnecessary transport layer's calls. This study work strategically (by incorporating certain functionalities) minimize such over calls.

By archiving the old location data (Manual or automated, this feature is not implemented in model application) overall system performance can be improved. Data rate can be reduced, by using data compression of SOAP messages [27], and a XML compression [28]. This reduces a network load, operational cost and increases the mobile Web Services performance. Data compression has implementation complexities and require more efficient mobile devices for decompression processing, That's why it has not been used in model application, in order to keep it simple. However, Author recommends to use data compression algorithms for optimized communication in LTCS.

2.5   Application Development Technologies

In this section author is intends to discuss about the possible application development technologies & environment for location tracking applications, and which one suit best for our purpose, and how it has been used for the development of model application.

There could be many possible platforms to develop such applications, including Java, Microsoft .Net and Arcview etc. But the intentions is to use an operating system independent tool, which should be an open source, and also supports SOAP based Web Services. Author will focus on Java related technologies in this study. Author has categorize the development tools into four separate areas, depending upon their functionality and relevance.

- *Java Development tools, NetBean IDE 6.0*:- The project uses Java EE5 Web Service, and NetBean 6.0 as java supported IDE, Netbean 6.0 is still in development phase so, intension was to testify new advantages of NetBean IDE, though its little unstable bust still fulfill the purpose, Sun application server 9.1 is used to deploy the tracking service and built in JavaDB is used as a DBMS.

- *Mapping, Geo coding and Location based services*:- In order to realize the location information on the Map, supervisor application module must use some sort of Map data source, from which it can extract Map images for certain coordinates and displays mobile units on them, or manages to trace a certain set or coordinates on the Map. There are many possibilities including Microsoft MapPoint .NET Web Service [29], Yahoo Map Service [30], Google Map Service [31] and ArcWeb Services [32]. May one can also manage own database but it would require tremendous cost and effort to collect all Map images, geocode them and to manage repositories. Each has its own implication and an implementation paradigm, this project utilizes

Google Map Services to visualize location information, and calculates textual routes, where as it uses Yahoo Map Service to extract Map image of a certain destination.

- *Supportive Java API's:-*

  o *J2ME Web Services APIs (WSA), JSR 172:-* Extend the Web Services platform to include J2ME. These J2ME Web Services APIs enable J2ME devices to be Web Services clients, providing a programming model that is consistent with the standard Web Services platform [33].

  o *Nokia Proposed JSR-179 Location API:-* For J2ME specification developed under the Java Community Process. This specification defines a J2ME Optional Package that enables mobile location-based applications for resource limited devices. The API is designed to be a compact and generic API that can produces information about the present geographic location of the terminal to Java applications. This API covers obtaining information about the present geographic location and orientation of the terminal and accessing a database of known landmarks stored in the terminal [33], there is an exclusive demo application available to demonstrate the capabilities of this API developed under NetBean IDE [34]. This project doesn't use this API because of unavailability of supportive equipment (Nokia E65, Sony Ericsson 990i), but it is highly recommended to use this API for such applications.

- *Testing Tools And Simulators:-* In order to test the developed model application author has used the Sun Java (TM) Wireless Toolkit 2.5.1 (A mobile device simulator tool that runs on the computer and provide the same operating conditions), and in order to simulate it in little more real conditions this project utilized WLAN enabled mobile phones with Symbion OS (Nokia E65 and Sony Ericsson 990i), Sony Ericsson 990i is less supportive and shows inconsistent behavior (losses connectivity unpredictably). HOLUX Slim236 Bluetooth enabled mouse used to collect location information, (See Appendix B) for more details.

2.6   Comparison of Existing Technologies & Applications

In this section the intention of the author is to provide, a technical comparison showing advantages and disadvantages of using different technologies vs. proposed one.

2.6.1 Operational Cost Estimation for Average Location Tracking System

The model application provides the basic functionality set for Location Tracking & Control System (LTCS), based on this set an initial rough cost has been estimated, that demonstrates if SMS protocol used instead of GPRS in this project then how it could has impact the over all operational cost for the system. Following table demonstrate provisional cost values for data amount (collected in lab environment) transported during a day session of 8 working hours with corresponding cost.

Table 3: Core functionalities of LTCS, amount of data needed for information exchange, and cost of data transfer.

Data rate using GPRS connection

Major Task	Kbytes Sent	Kbytes Received	Total KB	*{2}Cost(10KB=0.075Euro)	*{3}Formula per day cost	Operational cost per day (Euro)
Regular Position update	0.871	0.897	1.768	0.01	cost unit*3UpdatesPerMin*60minutes*8hours	14.4
*{1}A new job message receive	2.156	1.738	3.894	0.03	cost Unit*10AverageMessage	0.3
*{1}Textual direction pull	3.472	3.713	7.185	0.05	cost Unit*10AverageTextualDirectionPull	0.5
*{1}Map of destination pull	32.78	2.835	35.615	0.27	cost Unit*10AverageMapImagePull	2.7
Total	39.279	9.183	48.462	0.36		17.9

Data transfer using SMS

Major Task	SMS Sent	SMS Received	Total SMS	*{2}Cost(1SMS=0.19Euro and 1MMS=0.39Euro)	*{3}Formula per day cost	Operational cost per day (Euro)
Regular Position update	1	0	1	0.19	cost unit*3UpdatesPerMin*60minutes*8hours	273.6
*{1}A new job message receive	0	2	2	0.38	cost Unit*10AverageMessage	3.8
*{1}Textual direction pull	1	3	4	0.76	cost Unit*10AverageTextualDirectionPull	7.6
*{1}Map of destination pull	1	1	1SMS+1MMS	0.58	cost Unit*10AverageMapImagePull	5.8
Total	3	6	7	1.91		290.8

Conclusion is that GPRS will cost 6% of what SMS based system cost for same level of functionality!
*{1}Could vary depending on the size of contents, values are only rough estimates for average size.
*{2} Prices are only for O2 service provider specific, and could very company to company, also depends on the tariff and package used.
*{3}Its assumed there are 3 positional updates per minute (after each 20 seconds).
*More care use to be taken in SMS driven system in order to make communication only when desired (see Communication section above for more detail), because of the high cost and in GPRS/ICS based system even access of data exchange observed which justify its cost vs. functionality compromise.

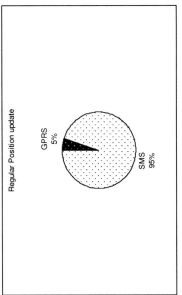

Figure 10: Impact on cost of regular position update.

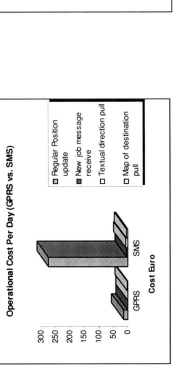

Figure 9: Operational cost comparison (GPRS vs. SMS).

Table 4: Comparison of existing Technologies & Applications.

Components of Interest	Available LTCS Using SMS	Available LTCS Using GPRS/ICS	Available LTCS Using Hybrid Techniques	Proposed LTCS
	Moderate	Moderate	High	Simple
Complexity How complex the architecture of the system is? Does it involve many modules? Requiring certain development, deployment and maintenance efforts.	• Server side SMS handling • Fleet management, multiple SMS centers • Data Pooling, delay management • Separating incoming data processing with business processing • Bigger fleet, requires extra hardware and software configuration • Separate database tier	• Dedicated Internet Link management • Multiple web content server, for bigger fleets • Separating incoming data processing with business processing • Bigger fleet, requires extra hardware and software configuration • Separate database tier	• Server side SMS handling • Fleet management, multiple SMS centers • Push proxy gateway management. • Dedicated Internet Link, management • Multiple web content server, for bigger fleets • Separating incoming data processing with business processing • Bigger fleet, requires extra hardware and software configuration • SMTP management • Separate database tier	• Dedicated Internet Link management • Single web content server • No separate database tier • Incoming data processing with business processing is handled by same server • Less configuration is required

Components of Interest	Available LTCS Using SMS	Available LTCS Using GPRS/ICS	Available LTCS Using Hybrid Techniques	Proposed LTCS
	Heavy	Heavy	Heavy	Light
Volume support How big the infrastructure of mobile units could be supported by such LTCS, for example *Eben-Azher* could have vehicle ranging between 10 to 15 which is reasonably moderate (model application would only take such load), but a commercial fleet could consist of hundreds of vehicles. Stronger servers with higher processing power would be required to cop the load of such big applications; also architectural strength would be an important factor.	• Support may vary for 10 to hundreds of mobile units • High count reflexes the stability of the system, for grater magnitude. • Commercial applications may vary from fleet management to, organizational resource management [35]. • Only allows interoperability in multiple applications if incorporated in design.	• Support may vary for 10 to hundreds of mobile units • High count reflexes the stability of the system, for grater magnitude. • Commercial applications may vary from fleet management to, organizational resource management [35]. • Only allows interoperability in multiple applications if incorporated in design.	• Support may vary for 10 to hundreds of mobile units • High count reflexes the stability of the system, for grater magnitude. • Commercial applications may vary from fleet management to, organizational resource management [35]. • Only allows interoperability in multiple applications if incorporated in design.	• Initially designed to take load of small fleet(10 to 30 vehicles) • Stable for small system. • Commercial applications may vary for small business vehicle tracking, mobile assets tracking and management. • Interoperable by design with other applications of smaller magnitude.

Components of Interest	Available LTCS Using SMS	Available LTCS Using GPRS/ICS	Available LTCS Using Hybrid Techniques	Proposed LTCS
	High	Moderate	High	Economical
Cost of setup (for 10 to 15 vehicle's fleet) Bigger system requires extra cost to deploy and setup the application. Such systems may require extra infrastructure, especial arrangements with service providers, dedicated servers, high speed internet, special hardware devices, customize equipment and additional software packages etc, every thing contribute into cost. Hardware requirement vary application to application, also the software technologies are dictated by the need of market, Open source license free solutions are cheaper but may require compromise with certain functionality/GUI requirements, and vise versa. This proposed solution is for small fleet and completely uses open source Java technologies. Which is cheaper and platform independent.	• Involve additional hardware cost for SMS processing on server side • Volume of application and infrastructure of organization determines the cost • Additional gateway and SMS center charges • Cellular network tariffs • Normally for small infrastructure could have ranges 5000 Euro to 10000 Euro, including equipment, related software's and connection fee [36]-[37] • Larger installations could have cost more then 10 of thousands Euros	• Involve GPRS connection charges, smaller connection setup fees, normally charged with amount of data transferred. • Volume of application and infrastructure of organization determines the cost • Normally for small infrastructure could have ranges 3000 Euro to 5000 Euro, including equipment, related software's and connection fees [37][39]. • Larger installations may not have a additional cost, but high speed access or more band width requirement could contribute extra cost	• Involve additional hardware cost for SMS processing on server side • Involve GPRS connection charges, smaller connection setup fees, normally charged with amount of data transferred • Volume of application and infrastructure of organization determines the cost • Additional gateway and SMS center charges. • Cellular network tariffs • Normally for small infrastructure could have ranges 5000 Euro to 10000 Euro, including equipment, related software's and connection fees [36][37][38],[40] • Larger installations could have cost more then 10 of thousands Euros. • High speed GPRS access or more band width requirement could contribute extra cost • Push proxy gateway service could possibly increase the cost	• Model application. Only for demonstration so no concrete cost involved, equipment borrowed form university lab • Involve GPRS connection charges, smaller connection setup fees, normally charged with amount of data transferred • High speed GPRS access or more band width requirement could contribute extra cost

Components of Interest	Available LTCS Using SMS	Available LTCS Using GPRS/ICS	Available LTCS Using Hybrid Techniques	Proposed LTCS
Hardware requirements (for 10 to 15 vehicle's fleet) Depending on the application area, some system may require especial customized hardware, for instance integrated GPS devices with GSM modem, special devices for SMS management at server side, certain processing units etc. (this study work uses simple standard Bluetooth enabled GPS mouse, a standard 3G mobile phone, and programmatically access positional data).	High • Specially designed integrated hardware with GPS & GSM SMS capabilities • Main frame servers, with high processing powers (2GHz, 2GB RAM) for each processing unit • Additional SMS receiving hardware is required on server side • Multiple SMS receiving units for parallel computing and delay control are required at server side	Moderate • Specially designed integrated hardware with GPS & GSM GPRS modem capabilities • Main frame servers, with high processing powers (2GHz, 2GB RAM) for each processing unit	High • Combination of specially designed integrated hardware with GPS & GSM SMS/GPRS modems or mobile phones, Email and WAP content receiving and displaying capabilities • Main frame servers, with high processing powers (2GHz, 2GB RAM) for each processing unit • Additional SMS receiving hardware is required on server side • Multiple SMS receiving units for parallel computing and delay control are required at server side • Additional server units for WAP proxy gateway	Low • No specially designed hardware needed. • Can use standard 3G mobile phones or PDA's with Bluetooth enabled GPS mouse. • Single server with high processing powers (2GHz, 2GB RAM).
Training requirements (for 10 to 15 vehicle's fleet users) There is always a need of training for application for respective users, but the complexity of the system increases the training requirements. The design of the application for certain users with certain background could also determine specific training requirements.	Moderate • Minimal training requirements for mobile workers, managing SMS alerts from the supervisor • Certain training requirements for supervisors at monitoring & control room (Understanding of web application and different functionalities, reports generation, Map reading etc.)	Moderate • Minimal training requirements for mobile workers, managing SMS alerts from supervisor • Certain training requirements for supervisors at monitoring & control room (Understanding of web application and different functionalities, reports generation, Map reading etc.)	Moderate • Special training requirements for mobile workers, handling WAP Push request interactions, managing and reading emails & SMS alerts • Certain training requirements for supervisors at monitoring & control room (Understanding of web application and different functionalities, reports generation, Map reading etc.)	Moderate • Minimal training requirements for mobile workers, an operating application at mobile device, which manages message and directional request • Certain training requirements for supervisors at monitoring & control room (Understanding of web application and different functionalities, reports generation, Map reading etc.)

Components of Interest	Available LTCS Using SMS	Available LTCS Using GPRS/ICS	Available LTCS Using Hybrid Techniques	Proposed LTCS
Flexibility Comes with the adoptability of the LTCS for varying application requirements and interoperability etc.	Maximum • Can be applied over diverse application areas (ranging from small to big business organizations)	Maximum • Can be applied over diverse application areas (ranging from small to big business organizations)	Maximum • Can be applied over diverse application areas (ranging from small to big business organizations)	Maximum • Can be applied over diverse application areas for small business organizations • Can be interchangeable deployed over WiFi enabled regions, without having extra cost, or even reduces the operational cost by avoiding GSM service provider • High interoperability brings greater marketing prospects
Operational cost of application (for 10 to 15 vehicle's fleet users) Operational cost for LTCS is determined by the service provider's charges, amount of data exchanged, design of the applications and requirement of certain functionalities.	High • Because of the high SMS cost, flat charges offered for certain applications, but compromise of functionalities and cost may vary organization to organization • Could be 290 Euro per mobile unit per day, if compared with same basic functionalities as model application (see section 1.5.1) • Continuous tracking on demand to cutoff price • Location query on demand to cutoff price.	Economical • 18 to 30 Euro per mobile unit per day. • Cost could boost with greater functional requirements	High • Because of the high SMS cost, flat charges offered for certain applications, but compromise of functionalities over cost may vary organization to organization • Could be 290 Euro per mobile unit per day, if compare with same basic functionalities as model application have (see section 1.5.1) • Continuous tracking on demand to cutoff price • Location query on demand to cutoff price • Additional cost for GPRS and WAP Push services	Economical • 18 Euro per mobile unit per day

Components of Interest	Available LTCS Using SMS	Available LTCS Using GPRS/ICS	Available LTCS Using Hybrid Techniques	Proposed LTCS
Tailoring of application for specific need The level of configurability of application also comes with cost. High customization requires more development effort to generalizes a solution. Model application is partially customizable as it could be implemented in any kind of tracking and control system. It could equally useful for planning a guided expeditions, and to monitoring mobile assets of any kind.	Customizable	Customizable	Customizable	Customizable
Communication technologies Author has discussed many communication possibilities, and have noticed that each have its own implication. It's the decision of fleet managers to choose the technology, which accommodate their business functionality needs with acceptable cost.	SMS / GSM (TCP/ IP for supervisor applications)	GPRS, HTTP and TCP/IP	SMS, GPRS, WAP Push, Email, HTTP, TCP/IP and GSM	(GPRS or WiFi), HTTP and TCP/IP
Amount of data exchanged for general operations (kilobytes)	Vary application to application	Vary application to application	Vary application to application	see section 1.5.1
Renting requirements for certain services or equipment	Vary application to application	Vary application to application	Vary application to application	No such Requirement

2.7   Summary

There could be many possibilities of data communication and development technologies. The objectives of the study work are to use a technology, which is maximum cost effective and extensible. Therefore this project work uses GPRS for data communication, since a virtual direct circuit is presented between the mobile device and the track server. It provides a quicker response time and enables the use of SOAP based Web Services under Java development platform. Furthermore a technological comparison shows that proposed model application is a cheaper but although it's equally workable choice (comparing other alternatives in market) for small and startup organizations.

3   Web Service Security

3.1   Overview

A location based data is a matter of high importance and sensitivity. The organizations operating such services may wish to make the data communication secure and foolproof.

This chapter will describe the security related issues of Web Services, what are the existing practices? what could be different security threats for location based data and what could be the possible remedies to overcome those threats.

The security of location based services depends on the strategies used by the service provider and the principal user, there is no hard and fast rule but there are certain guidelines that could be followed as explained in subsequent sections.

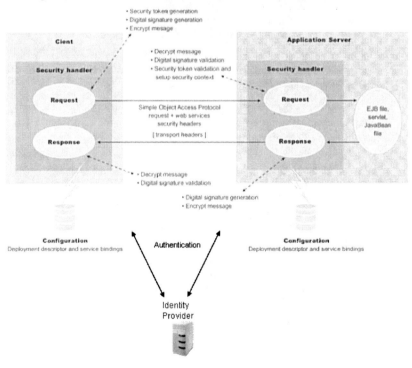

Figure 11: Web Service security architecture [48].

3.2   Security Requirements for Location Based Data

There is a need to securely gather and the transfer location information for route tracking and control services, while at the same time protecting the privacy of the individuals. The collection and transfer of the location information about a particular target can be an important privacy implication. There is a need of protocol to facilitate the protection of privacy pursuant to Privacy Rules set by the "user/owner of the Target". The ability to gather and generate a target's location and access to a derived location, are key elements of the location-based services privacy equation. Central to a target's privacy are (a) the identity of entities that have access to raw location data, derived location, and/or have access to derived location information, and (b) whether those entities can be trusted to know and follow the Privacy Rules of the user [47]. The main principles to guide the requirements could be described as:

1. Security of the transmission of Location Object is an essential to guarantee the integrity and confidentiality of the location information. This includes authenticating the sender and receiver of the Location Object and securing the Location Object.

2. A critical role is played by user-controlled Privacy Rules, which describe the restrictions imposed or permissions given by the "Rule Maker". The Privacy Rules specify the necessary conditions that allow a Location Server to forward Location Information to a Location Recipient, and the conditions and purposes for that the Location Information can be used.

3. One type of Privacy Rules specifies how location information should be filtered, depending on who the recipient is. Filtering is the process of reducing the precision or resolution of the data. A typical rule may be of the form: "my location can only be disclosed to the owner of such credentials in such precision or resolution" (e.g., "my co-workers can be told the city I am currently in") [47].

3.3   Security Standards

The location based applications that involve Web Services, most of the security related issues discussed above could be addressed to by following the recommendation and adopting the practices proposed for securing Web Services. Following is a brief discussion about available standards and how they could be used for this study work.

3.3.1 Liberty Alliance (Identity and Web Services)

In today's information economy, trust is the necessary foundation for secure interoperability, and central to the successful realization of what's possible on the Web.

From the user perspective as well as of the deploying organization, it's an issue of who is trusted with what and that requires policy, business and technology understanding and infrastructure. This becomes the reason for the Liberty Alliance project, which is a first-of-its-kind standards organization with a global membership that provides a holistic approach to identity [45]-[46].

For instance driver of mobile unit registered to *Eben-Ezer* wants to use a service by third party *GPSTrackingServer.* but *Eben-Ezer* and *GPSTrackingServer* don't know each other. In a same way control manager at *Eben-Ezer* want to track registered mobile units, using the service provided by third party *GPSTrackingServer*, but *GPSTrackingServer* organization don't know *Eben-Ezer* and its users. It is not possible for *GPSTrackingServer* organization to keep the information of all prospective client companies and their users into database. So now there is a company (*Liberty Alliance*) a global organization which provides the security warranty services, both *Eben-Ezer* and *GPSTrackingServer* registerd with Liberty Alliance. When a user of *Eben-Ezer* want some service from *GPSTrackingServer*, it first goes to *Liberty Alliance* and requests for a Security Token, it takes that token, attach it to request message and dispatch it to *GPSTrackingServer*. *GPSTrackingServer* requests *Liberty Alliance* for the authentication, *Liberty Alliance* verify and provide warranty that the request is from valid user of a registered company. *GPSTrackingServer* provides the desired service to the user.

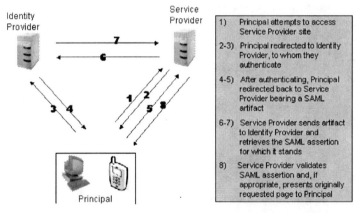

Figure 12: Conceptual illustration of Liberty Alliance role [46] .

The location tracking and control applications could enable a mobile user to enjoy diverse facilities by becoming a part of such open source services. Many organization or companies may interact with same mobile user to facilitate while he/she is on move. This could vary from pizza delivery to the nearest emergency rescue station, employee or vehicle tracking to advertisement of user profile specific artifacts. Liberty Alliance could act as a trusted party to ensure reliable interaction among several parties. In this study work for the sake of simplicity the GPSTrackingServer know Eben-Ezer and its users so the middle layer of Liberty Alliance could be avoided.

3.3.2 OASIS WS-Security Standard Specification

The OASIS WS-Security specification is a part of the Advancement of the Structured Information Standards (OASIS). Its purpose is to establish a conman framework for SOAP based Web Services security to achieve reliable interoperability between applications. The study report cited a part of the specification to develop the reader's understanding for the context, because the model application has adopted a part of the proposed security model.

This specification provides three main mechanisms [44], ability to send security token as a part of a message, message integrity, and message confidentiality. But these mechanisms do not provide a complete security solution for Web Services. Instead, this specification is a building block that can be used in conjunction with other Web Service extensions and higher-level application-specific protocols to accommodate a wide variety of security models and security technologies. This study work has adopted the guide lines for the security token part for message integrity. The message confidentiality feature could be added in future work.

When securing SOAP messages, various types of threats should be considered. Those may includes the following:

- The message could be modified or read by attacker.

- An antagonist could send well-formed messages to a service, that lack the appropriate security claims to warrant processing.

- An antagonist could alter a message to the service which being well formed causes the service to process and respond to the client for an incorrect request.

To understand these threats this specification defines a message security model [44] which consist of the following,

1) Message Security Model

This standard specifies an abstract message security model in terms of security tokens combined with digital signatures to protect and authenticate SOAP messages.

Security tokens assert claims and could be used to assert the binding between authentication secrets/keys and security identities.

Signatures are used to verify the message origin and its integrity. Signatures are also used by message producers to demonstrate a knowledge of the key, typically from a third party, used to confirm the claims in a security token and thus to bind their identity (and any other claims occurring in the security token) to the messages they have created [44].

2) Message Protection

Protecting the message content from being disclosed (confidentiality) or modified without detection (integrity) are primary security concerns. This specification provides a means to protect a message by encrypting and/or digitally signing a body, a header, or any combination of them or parts of them.

3) Invalid or Missing Claims

A message recipient should reject the messages containing invalid signatures, the messages missing necessary claims or messages whose claims have unacceptable values. Such messages are unauthorized (or malformed). This part discussed here for reader interest, but it have not been implemented in this study work. This specification provides a flexible way for the message producer to make a claim about the security properties by associating zero or more security tokens with the message. An example of a security claim is the identity of the producer; the producer can claim that he is Bob, known as an employee of some company, and therefore he has the right to send the message [44].

3.4 Summary

There could be varity of ways to securing the location based Web Services. As the intension of this study work is to demonstrate a model application for proof of concept. The technique adopted in this study work, is an application which generates a simple security token at server side at the time user logged-in, and then maintained it as a mean of authentication for each message, thorough out the session between tracking server, monitoring supervisor and mobile unit.

4   Model Application for Proof of Concept

4.1   Overview

This chapter presents the architectural prospective of the proposed system. It covers the design concepts of the system, possible alternatives, advantages of chosen technology and details of the constructs, of the model application, which based on UML modeling.

4.2   Actors and General Tracking & Control Application Components

In order to understand the requirements of different stake holders for tracking and control system, a brief hallucination with minimum set of features could be demonstrated as follow,

4.2.1 Mobile Worker Carrying Mobile Phone and GPS Device

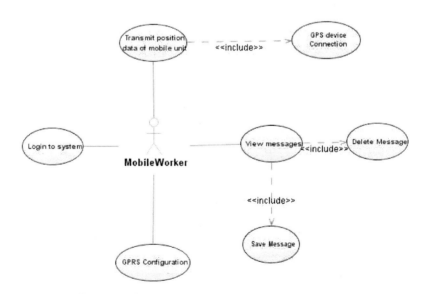

Figure 13: Use cases from mobile worker prospective.

4.2.2 Supervisor of Tracking & Control Application

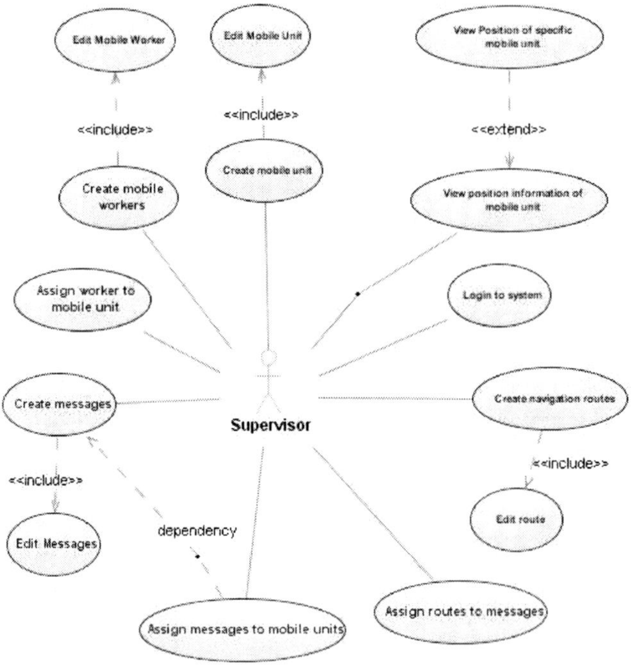

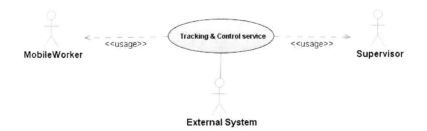

Figure 14: Use cases from supervisor prospective.

4.2.3 External Systems Wanted to Avail Services in Either Role

Figure 15: Use cases from external system prospective.

Generally Tracking & Control system could be decomposed into three distinct components,

- An application running on mobile device collects and transmits GPS based positional data.

- A technology on the track server end that receives location data, facilitate storage, manipulation, and communicate control instructions back to mobile units in the field.

- A supervisor application to control and monitor the set of mobile units, using track server and its database.

The approach to exchange the information between mobile unit and control room is the point of interest in this study work.

4.3   Different Possibilities

To realize a tracking system, updating positional information, receiving messages, textual directions and Map images for the destination, requires a mean to communicate the data. There are different possibilities like SMS, WAP Push, GPRS, SOAP messages, and email etc. (See chapter 2). On the other hand in order to visually render such information for the application there are also many possibilities, including our own spatial Mapping database or third party databases like Google Map Service, Yahoo Map Service, Microsoft Map point etc. (See chapter 2).

Nature of the required application determines the technology that suits the purpose in a best way (See chapter 2). Proposed architecture should be cost effective, flexible, extensible, portable and the security & privacy of the location information are guaranteed across the network.

Background of architectural requirements:-

- One data character is represented by 8 bits, which is one byte in size.

- SMS are of fix size (160 character mean 160 bytes) and fix cost has charged by service provider for each SMS (See chapter 2)..

- GPRS data packets are of variable length and are charged in terms of amount of data uploaded or downloaded over the network (See chapter 2).

- Typical GPS location data consists of Longitude, Latitude and UTC Time, which is also of fixed size in terms of characters, for a certain level of precision.

    o Latitude: 5200.9657/ (9 Bytes)

    o Longitude: 00854.2983 (10 Bytes)

    o UTC Time: 202229.708 (10 Bytes)

- o   29 character or 29 bytes altogether.

- Where as the textual directional data could be of variable size, generally influenced by the distance between two points, the number of intersections in the way and local naming conventions for streets or roads.

- The size of MAP images could also be variable and mostly depends on the dimension and image format. For this study we could consider the size of the directional Map image of 300X 309 pixel dimension of PNG format is 30 Kbytes approximately.

- The size of messages explaining the job description would depend on the nature of job and desire level of explanation by individuals, so this is also variable. It could be as short as few characters or as long as few lines exceeding 160 characters.

- The cost factor for any instance of time during the operational system, would be directly related to the size of the data that has to transfer between nodes.

- Operational cost of the overall system is a collective cost, for each data transaction.

The following section sums the different architectural possibilities, and their operational cost. The chosen architecture should be more flexible towards the individual data transaction cost.

4.3.1 Using Only SMS Technology for Two Way Data Communication

SMS is designed to deliver short bursts of data such as numerical pages, to avoid overloading the system with more than the standard forward-and-response operation, the inventors of SMS agreed on a 160-character maximum message size.

Regular location data is very less then the available capacity of SMS data packet, on the other hand occasionally there might be a need of more capacity to send longer directional messages, that could be done by partitioning data into multiple messages, which will be a compromise of SMS cost and latency.

This technology needs more hardware on server side that could enable the server to send messages over the dedicated link, or receive messages from different mobile units, queue them for updating and processing.

Cellular network service providers charge fixed price for each SMS, even though small data exchange would adhere the needless cost (See Chapter 2).

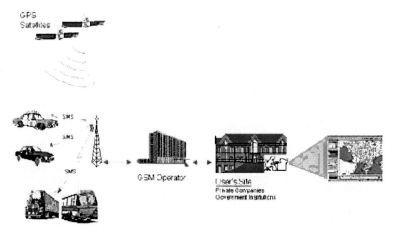

Figure 16: Using SMS for data exchange [39].

4.3.2 Using Hybrid Technologies (SMS, WAP Push and Email)

An other architectural possibility is to use hybrid scheme. For example location data could be send via SMS because of its small nature, where as the textual messages or Map images could be send to mobile unit via email, alerts for new mails to the mobile units could be sent via WAP Push. It could also be the other way around.

This methodology on the one way gives an open, flexible and extensible architecture. On the other hand it involves more user interaction as needed in many tracking applications. Again using SMS involve compromise because either it provides more then or less then required data capacity.

There could be some optimal techniques to over come such type of issues, by introducing a dynamic switching mechanism in order to determine which technique should be used for a specific data transfer. It will involve additional hardware its deployment and maintenance. It makes system more complex, and there will be a compromise between the flexibility and cost.

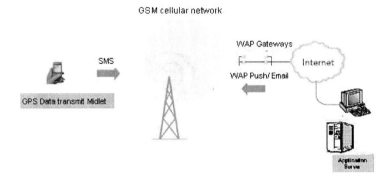

Figure 17: Using hybrid technologies for data exchange.

4.3.3 Using GPRS, Data Packets, SOAP Messages via Web Service

This architecture supports variable data communication, and provides room to strategically reduce the data size, so the cost effect could be reduced. Because system operational cost is depend on the total amount of data exchanged.

A great advantage is its flexibility, that allows system to exist even if GPRS modem layer replaced by WLAN. The system is equally effective and deployable using the advantage of WiFi environment, already functional in some parts of the world like Paris and London. Because of its flexibility (See Chapter 2), this approach is used to develop a model application, proposed in this study work.

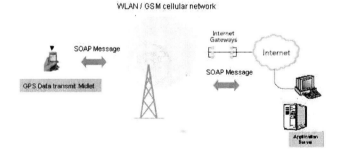

Figure 18: Using GPRS data packets for data exchange.

4.4   Proposed Architecture & Its Design

The use of GPRS data packets are more cost effective than the other data transfer techniques (as described previously), that's why the project is based on GPRS data packets and uses SOAP messages realized by Web Service for data exchange. There may be some other possibilities like Java server pages or servlets to realize the application but Web Services use the SOAP messages (based on XML) and more flexible to integrate with the third parties. This section discusses the general architecture of the system along with its integral parts.

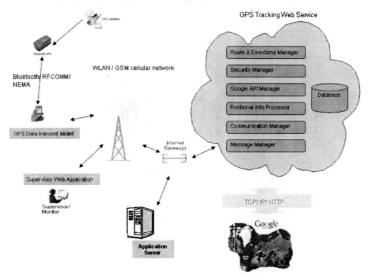

Figure 19: General summary architectural view.

There will be three major components residing on different tiers, which communicates each other and to external services using SOAP messages to realize the complete system.

- GPS data transmitter application:- This component resides on mobile device, collects the positioning data from Bluetooth enabled GPS device, maintains the connection and transmits the data to the GPS Tracking & Control Web Service after a regular interval. It also receives and display supervisor messages to the mobile worker who holds mobile device. GPS connection is realized as a one way message communication, in which data flows from GPS mouse to the mobile device using Bluetooth RFCOMM protocol, and the format of the positional data is specified by NMEA standard sentences.

- Supervisor web application:- This component is hosted on a web server, realized as presentation layer based on Java Server Pages, and a business logic layer provided by a Web Service. It should allow to setup new mobile units and workers, binds them together, facilitate them creating routes and messages. It assigns new messages to the mobile workers, facilitate to display the position information, track mobile units, allow view some important reports and communicates with Google Map API for visualizations.

- GPS tracking Web Service:- It is a core of the system, hosted by web server at a separate tier. It should be responsible to process, coordinate and manage location tracking data among transmitter unit and the control room. It will exchange XML based SOAP messages to realize the data communication.

Google Map Service API is consumed to visualize the positional information and allows to make new directional routes.

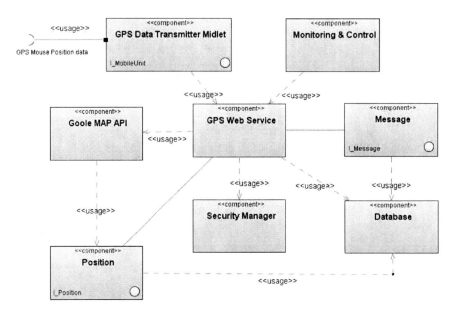

Figure 20: System components diagram.

Figure 20 shows all the design components of the model application, some important components have been detailed in subsequent section.

GPS Data Transmitter Midlet

Responsible to communicate with GPS device and
transmit position, pull messages and route directions

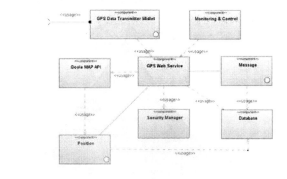

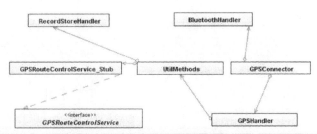

- *GPSConnector:-* System uses this class as a presentation GUI. This class communicate with business logic classes and realize the complete mobile application for transmitting the positional data.
- *GPSHandler:-* System uses this class to connect and communicate with GPS device and to process and transmit position data after regular intervals, the same class monitors the incoming messages and intimate user.
- *BlutoothHandler:-* System uses this class to discover and list the available Bluetooth devices along with their Bluetooth address. The information collected by this class used for configuration of the mobile application to communicate with selected GPS mouse.
- *RecordStoreHandler:-* System uses this class to store the messages and their status locally on the mobile phone. This class provides DBMS functionality for mobile unit.
- *UtilMethods:-* System uses this class as a core utility factory, which enables each part of the application to communicate together and also to the web service. This class provide all operations for data formatting and display.
- *GPSRouteControlService_Stub:-* System uses this class as a stub (client) for the Web service. This class used to process all the transmission and control related SOAP messages from web service.
- *GPSRouteControlService:-* This is a utility class, act as interface for web service stub class.

Figure 21: GPS data transmitter class diagram.

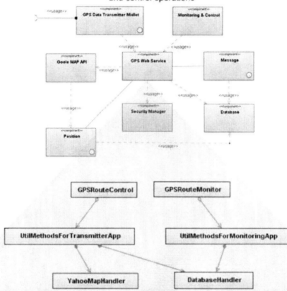

- **GPSRouteControl:-** System uses this class to enable mobile client, for updating positional data, pulling messages, textual routes, Maps etc.
- **GPSRouteMonitor:-** System uses this class to enable monitoring application to monitor, track and control registered mobile units. Generate reports, perform system setup creating messages and new routes.
- **UtilMeithodsForTranmitterApp:-** System uses this class as core utility factory for GPS Route Control service to mobile client. This class process all business logic, communicate with database, provide security related features, create textual route, and map images etc.
- **UtilMethodForMonitorApp:-** System uses this class as core utility factory for Monitoring service to supervisor client. This class process all business logic , database communication, and produce visualization related data to facilitate Google Map Service.
- **YahooMapHandler:-** System uses this class to communicate with Yahoo Map Service to produce destination map images.
- **DatabaseHandler:-** System uses this class to manages database. This class is responsible to execute all queries, communicate results to other functional classes. Purpose of this class is to manage code by separating database related operations from business logic.

Figure 22: GPS Web Service class diagram.

Monitoring & Control

Responsible to create visualizations for the supervisor to
monitor, track and control mobile units

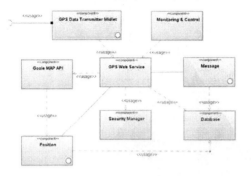

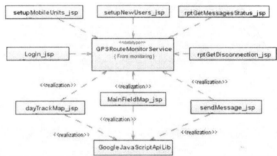

- *MainFieldMap:-* System uses this class to display map of field area with all mobile units marked with their current location.
- *dayTrackMap:-* System uses this class to display the track of specific mobile unit over the map for given certain interval.
- *senMaessage:-* System uses this class to send directional messages with job description, and allow to visualize intended route.
- *GPSRouteMonitorService:-* System uses this class as an interface to the web service. This facilitate all business logic and data processing
- *GoogleJavaScriptApiLib:-* System uses this class as core unit, which enables application to visualization all Maps related data. This class communicate with Google API and process geographical data.
- *Setup MobileUnits and NewUsers:-* System uses these classes for registration and management of new mobile unit and system users.
- *rptGetDisconnection:-* System uses this class to generate disconnection time report for specific mobile unit.
- *rptGetMessagesStatus:-* System uses this class to generate report for messages sent to mobile units, their status and descriptions.

Figure 23: Monitoring & Control application class diagram.

Google Map API

Provide services for mapping and geocoding ,on map
drawing tools, directional maps and text

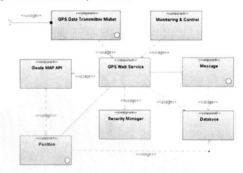

Following are few java script functions, created to manipulate Google Map API in the context of Project work.

- *loadAndDisplayMarkers:-* System uses this function to load the field Map and mark all mobile units on it.
- *Refresh:-* System uses this function to refresh the field Map after specific interval. This application call the function after one minute.
- *drawMarker:-* System uses this function to draw the marker with description of mobile unit.
- *Track:-* System uses this function to draw the connected route of positions for a mobile unit, collected from database via web service.
- *GetTextiualRoute:-* System uses this function to calculate the the textual route between two points.

The Google classes used to achieve above functionalities are (Gdirections, GMap2, Gmarker, Gpolyline, Gicon, GLatLng)

Figure 24: Google Map Service API and related classes.

4.5   Aspects of Interest

The objective of this section is to give the user a good engineering prospective of the developed application. In order to keep it simple and more understandable, only those sub components of any major aspect will be discussed with an optimum level of detail, those have significant contribution in the realization of proposed tracking & control system.

The application has been broken down into several aspects which contribute as the building blocks for the application. Following areas are covered while discussing each aspect in detail,

- Design goals that would explain the required aspect's objective & its importance into the system.

- Inner components are the individual tasks, which together realize the aspect.

- Data flow will be demonstrated in terms of use case documentation, that explains the exchange of messages between components, users and external systems.

- Related GUI's of the developed application.

- Design and implementation section presents the UML modeling for the inner components of that specific aspect of system. This section mostly contains the sequence diagrams and class diagrams. There are some important code segments that would also be included to demonstrate the applied algorithm. In order to keep the explanation simple to understand modeling is meant to be of abstract level.

The aspects discussed in the sub sequent section are in chronological order.

4.5.1 Receive & Transmit Location Data via Mobile Transmitter Application

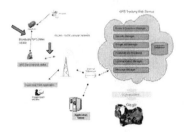

The design goal of this aspect is to communicate with the GPS device and to receive a special formatted data, parses it and extracts the useful positioning information, and then transmits this information to the tracking Web Service, which would update it into the database.

The data communication technology is based on Bluetooth, so it will involve the discovery of the GPS devices and then makes a connection to a particular device, to get the data in NEMA format.

This aspect of the proposed application could be further divided into following tasks,

- Bluetooth GPS mouse discovery and connection.
- Regular update of position data via Web Service to track server.

Use Case Name:	Bluetooth GPS mouse discovery and connection
Actors:	Mobile Worker
Trigger:	When ever mobile unit gets operational first time.
Description:	This use case will happen when ever mobile unit gets operational first time, mobile worker will configure the Bluetooth device address of the GPS mouse and position update interval. That stored locally into mobile device and will be used next time for communication. Mobile worker logins to the system and request for the list of Bluetooth devices. Selects the GPS mouse attached or provided with mobile phone or PDA to configure the application, and then connects to the configured GPS device.
Preconditions:	1. Mobile Worker's identity has been authenticated. 2. Mobile unit has sufficient free memory available to start the task. 3. GPS mouse is a Bluetooth enabled and working properly.
Post conditions:	1. connect to GPS device and start sending positional data
Normal Flow 1:	1. Mobile worker will request the list of Bluetooth devices. 2. Application will perform device discovery and generates a list of available devices, and displays it to the user. 3. Mobile worker will select the specific device and requests to save. 4. System will save configuration data. 5. Mobile worker request to connect.

	6. System connect with configured GPS device.
Alternative Flow 1:	1. Mobile worker would request to connect with GPS.
	2. System will connect to pre configured GPS device.
Exceptions:	3. No GPS mouse found.
	4. Mobile phone discharged.
Actions for Exceptions:	1. Display appropriate error message.
	2. Execute the use case again, after ensuring GPS mouse working properly.
Frequency of Use:	Very often! One of the central use case for the system.
Assumptions:	System works in ideal conditions.
Notes and Issues:	System is implemented in laboratory environment so the limitations could be observed. Task implemented as working prototype with basic features.

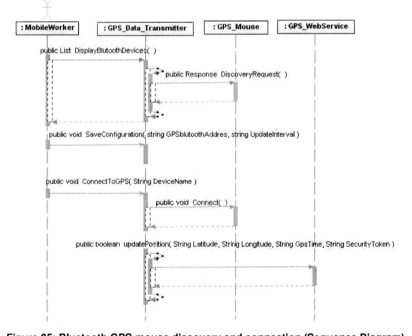

Figure 25: Bluetooth GPS mouse discovery and connection (Sequence Diagram).

Figure 26: Bluetooth GPS mouse discovery and connection (GUI).

Use Case Name:	Regular update of position data via Web Service to track server.
Actors:	GPS Transmitter Application.
Trigger:	When ever mobile unit login and connect to the GPS device.
Description:	This use case will happen when ever the mobile unit connects to the provided GPS device. It will start sending positional information automatically until application turn off or mobile unit logoff.
Preconditions:	1. Mobile Worker's identity has been authenticated. 2. Mobile unit has sufficient free memory available to launch task. 3. Connection with the GPRS is established. 4. Connection with the GPS mouse is established. 5. Track server is up and running. 6. Web Service has deployed, and application has the valid reference of it.
Post conditions:	1. Positional data should be available on track server.
Normal Flow:	1. Mobile unit will call update positional data method of the Web

	Service.
	2. Web Service will update the position information into database and check for the new messages.
	3. Web Service would inform the availability of message status to the mobile unit.
	4. If there is no new message then Alternative flow 1.
	5. Mobile unit continue sending positional data updates.
	6. Web Service updates the current positional information in database.
Alternative Flows:	1. Reference use case "View the supervisor messages contain directional information".
Exceptions:	2. GPRS connection breakup.
	3. Web server stopped responding.
	4. GPS mouse stop responding.
Actions for Exceptions:	1. Maintain log at server for disconnection period.
	2. Display appropriate error message.
	3. Restart of the application recommended.
Frequency of Use:	Very often! basic use case for the system.
Special Requirements:	Use case should overcome the exceptions, minimize the disconnection period.
Assumptions:	System works in ideal conditions.
Notes and Issues:	System is implemented in laboratory environment, to observe the limitations. Task is implemented as working prototype with basic features.

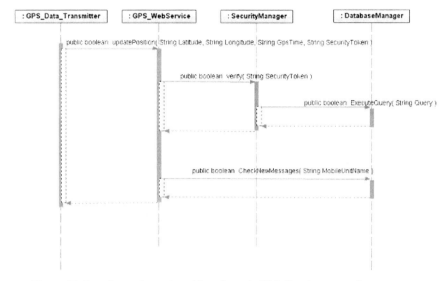

Figure 27: Regular update of position data via Web Service to track server (Sequence Diagram).

Figure 28: Regular update of position data via Web Service to track server (GUI).

4.5.2 Instructional Messages Handling

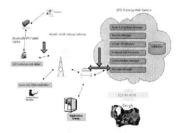

The design goal of this component is to enable the two ways messaging between Web Service and a mobile unit. In first version of the application the supervisor could send the textual instruction of new jobs. And mobile unit can accept the messages read them and update their status to the control room.

This aspect may be further sub divided into tasks, effected area by this aspect showed with red arrows in system understanding diagram discussed before (See Section 4.4), is listed as,

- Message sending by monitoring application

- Message pulling by mobile unit

Use Case Name:	Send the Message to the mobile unit in field.
Actors:	Supervisor.
Trigger:	When ever there is a need to direct mobile unit to a new destination to perform some job.
Description:	This use case will trigger when ever the supervisor need to send a message to any specific mobile unit. The message will contain the job description and the directional information. When supervisor request for the send message GUI. System will show a screen having input controls, which requests message name, and description, destination address. After successful completion of data input form, supervisor can optionally visualize the driving direction through Google Map Service. After creating message supervisor could press the send button, System will create message and change, this will allow mobile user able to pull the message.
Preconditions:	1. Supervisor's identity has been authenticated. 2. Application Server is running.

	3. Connection with the internet is established.
Post conditions:	1. Message should be created and status should be set as pull able.
Normal Flow:	2. Supervisor will select mobile unit from the drop down provided on main control screen. 3. Supervisor will push button send new message on main control screen. 4. System will display new message GUI. 5. Supervisor will fill the message name, description, destination address in the input fields. 6. Optionally, if supervisor press the view direction button then Alternative flow 1. 7. Supervisor could press the send button and Web Service will create the message and change its status in database.
Alternative Flows:	1. The direction from current position of the mobile unit to the desired address will be displayed through Google Map driving direction API.
Exceptions:	1. Web server stopped responding.
Actions for Exceptions:	Prompt error message to the user.
Frequency of Use:	Very often! central use case for the system.
Assumptions:	System works in ideal conditions.
Notes and Issues:	System is implemented in laboratory environment, to observe the limitations. Task is implemented as working prototype with basic features.

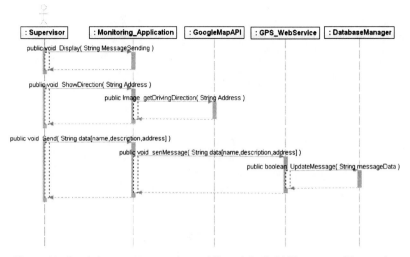

Figure 29: Send the message to the mobile unit in field (Sequence Diagram).

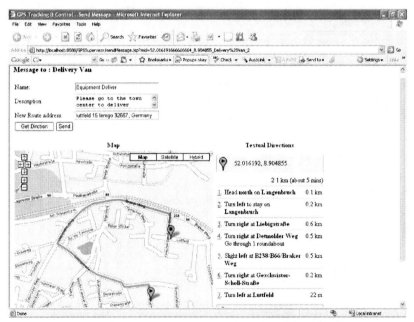

Figure 30: Send the message to the mobile unit in field (GUI).

Use Case Name:	Message pulling by mobile unit.
Actors:	Mobile Worker.
Trigger:	When ever supervisor creates a new directional message and assigns it to the mobile unit.
Description:	This use case will happen when ever there is a new message for the mobile worker. Every time mobile unit update the positional information to the Web Service, Web Service will check for the new messages for that mobile unit and return availability status. Based on that status the mobile unit will trigger the pull new message service request, and display returned message to the mobile worker.
Preconditions:	1. Mobile Worker's identity has been authenticated. 2. Mobile device has sufficient free memory available to launch task. 3. Connection with the GPRS is established.
Post conditions:	Message status should be changed into read.
Normal Flow:	1. Mobile unit will call the update positional data method of the Web Service. 2. Web Service will update the position information into database and check for the new messages. 3. Web Service will inform the new message availability status to the mobile unit. 4. If there is no new message then Alternative flow 1. 5. If there are new message then a mobile unit will send the pull message request to the Web Service. 6. Web Service wil return the un read message. 7. Application will alert the mobile worker and display the new message. 8. Mobile unit will send the acknowledgement to the Web Service. 9. Web Service updates the message status in database.
Alternative Flows:	1. mobile unit continue sending position updates.
Exceptions:	1. GPRS connection breakup.

	2. Web server stopped responding. 3. Mobile battery discharged. 4. GPS mouse battery discharged. 5. System hanged up.
Actions for Exceptions:	Maintain log at server for disconnection period of the mobile unit.
Frequency of Use:	Very often! central use case for the system.
Special Requirements:	Use case should overcome the exceptions, and QoS issues.
Assumptions:	System works in ideal conditions.
Notes and Issues:	System is implemented in laboratory environment, to observe the limitations. Task is implemented as working prototype with basic features.

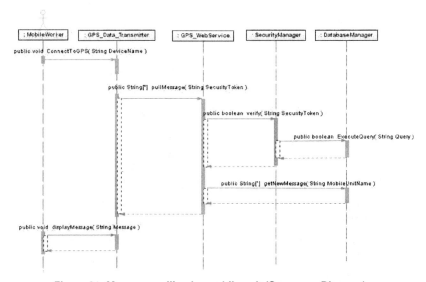

Figure 31: Message pulling by mobile unit (Sequence Diagram).

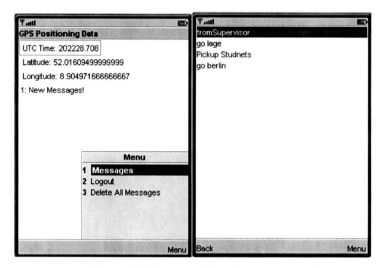

Figure 32: Message pulling by mobile unit (GUI).

4.5.3 Textual Direction

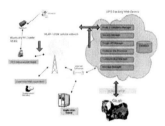

The design goal of this component is to send a request for the textual route information to the Web Service, and pull the recommended route plan and display that at the mobile device screen.

The purpose of this aspect is to estimate the route direction from the current location of mobile unit, to the destination. In application, this is achieved through using a third party component "IMozillaBrowserCanvas", which renders the contents of the JavaScript provided by Google Map API. That script is embedded into a JSP page, which gets the dynamic route information as demonstrated by flowing code segment.

```
URL=http://HostServer/GPSTrackerWebservice/getTextDirection.jsp?from=detmold,Ge
rmany&to=52.02287071170068,8.894977569580078&routeID=1;

IMozillaBrowserCanvas BROWSER = BrowserFactory.spawnMozilla();

BROWSER.loadURL(URL);

BROWSER.addNetworkListener( new NetworkAdapter() {

    public void onDocumentComplete(NetworkEvent e) {

    BROWSER.selectAll();

    retRouteVal=BROWSER.getSelectedText();

    updateTextualRouteDetail(""+retRouteVal+"",routeID);

    }

});
```

Use Case Name:	Request & display the textual route.
Actors:	Mobile Worker.
Trigger:	When ever there is a need of detailed guidance for the destination.
Description:	This use case will happen when ever mobile worker need to know the route plan for the destination. Mobile worker will send the request to the Web Service. It provides the route id already attached with the specific job message. Web Service will request the Google's *Geocoding* service to supply textual route, which would then stored in database to allow mobile unit to pull the directional route and display to the mobile worker.
Preconditions:	1. Mobile worker identity has been authenticated. 2. Application Server is running. 3. Connection with the internet is established.
Post conditions:	1. Textual route should be displayed on the screen of mobile unit.
Normal Flow:	1. Mobile worker will select the "Get Direction Text" menu command from the message detail screen. 2. Mobile application will send the request to the Web Service and provides selected message id. 3. Web Service will request the Google Geocoding service, to collect the information and store it into database. 4. Mobile application will pull the textual route plan from Web Service.

	5. Mobile application will display the route information on the screen.
Exceptions:	2. Web server stopped responding. 3. Google API doesn't respond. 4. Proxy configuration for IMozillaBrowser are incorrect.
Actions for Exceptions:	Prompt error message to the user.
Frequency of Use:	Often.
Assumptions:	System works in ideal conditions.
Notes and Issues:	System is implemented in laboratory environment, to observe the limitations. Task is implemented as working prototype with basic features.

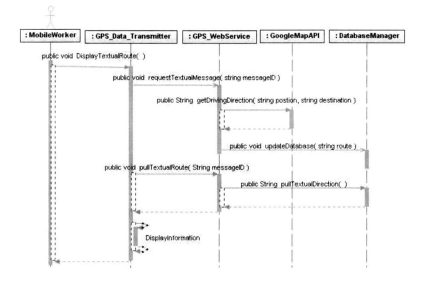

Figure 33: Request & display the textual route (Sequence Diagram).

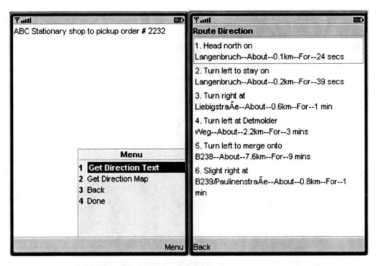

Figure 34: Request & display the textual route (GUI).

4.5.4 Graphical (Map) Direction

The design goal of this aspect is to request the destinations Map from the Web Service and display it at mobile unit screen.

This functionality is achieved by using Yahoo Map API Service. Format of URL that request for a Map image is as follow,

"http://api.local.yahoo.com/MapsService/V1/mapImage?appid="+YAHOO_API_KE
Y+"&location="+location+"&image_height=309&image_width=300&zoom=4"

The response of above URL will returns the reference URL of created PNG Map image, which would later used by mobile unit to download actual image.

The image is consist of the Map of the surrounded area with destination marked as (*).

Use Case Name:	Request & display the destination Map.
Actors:	Mobile Worker.
Trigger:	When ever there is a need of Map of the destination.
Description:	This use case will happen when ever the mobile worker needs to see the Map of the destination. Mobile worker will send the request to the

	Web Service, and provides the route id attached with the specific job message. message. Web Service will request the Yahoo Map API to create Map image of desired area. Yahoo Map Service would create image and return the URL to access that image's PNG file. That URL will be used by mobile unit to download image directly form Yahoo Map Server, and then display that to the user.
Preconditions:	1. Mobile worker identity has been authenticated. 2. Application Server is running. 3. Connection with the internet is established.
Post conditions:	1. Map should be displayed on the screen of mobile unit with destination marked as (*).
Normal Flow:	1. Mobile worker will select the "Get Direction Map" menu command from the message detail screen. 2. Mobile application will send the request to the Web Service, by providing selected message id. 3. Web Service will request the Yahoo Map Service to generate Map image and return its reference URL. 4. Mobile application will download the image URL, and then directly connect to the Yahoo Map Service and download Map image. 5. Mobile application will display the Map on the screen.
Exceptions:	1. Web server stopped responding. 2. Yahoo Map API doesn't respond.
Actions for Exceptions:	Prompt error message to the user.
Frequency of Use:	Often.
Assumptions:	System works in ideal conditions.
Notes and Issues:	As an initial study, only the destination is marked, future is work required to display the driving direction graphically on the downloaded Map.

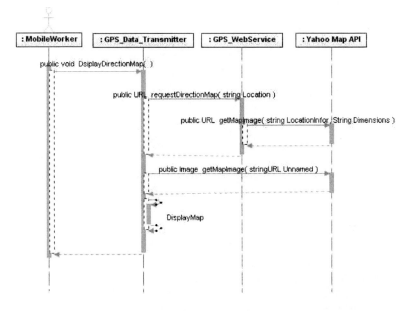

Figure 35: Request & display the destination Map (Sequence Diagram).

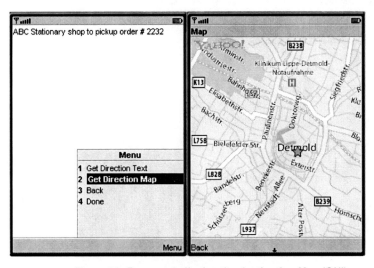

Figure 36: Request & display the destination Map (GUI).

4.5.5 Monitoring & Control

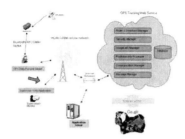

The objective of this aspect is to allow supervisors to monitor & control the mobile units in the field. Normally there use to be a big screen in a control stations, which displays the Map of the region (in web browser), and display the current location of the each mobile unit in the field. The supervisor's application refreshes itself each minute to reflex real-time locations of all the mobile units.

This functionality is achieved by making use of a JSP based web application. That uses Google Map API to display Maps, and all the registered mobile units along with their locations. The main GUI is a JSP page, that have a MAP of the field with control options. Those options includes the mobile unit tracking, message sending, generation of reports, and setup for mobile units and system users. The application displays the most latest location (in database) of each mobile unit.

A dropdown (option, input GUI control) on the top left part of the screen will allow supervisor to select any particular mobile unit, to perform its related monitoring & control operations.

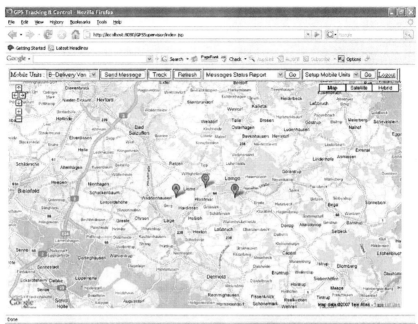

Figure 37: Location data monitoring application (GUI).

4.5.6 Mobile Unit Tracking

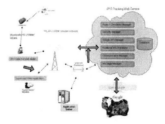

These aspects will allow the supervisor to track the directed route followed by a mobile unit, between any specific time interval. The GUI is on a JSP page that interacts with the Google API, which draws polylines to make a connected plot of direction.

The default-tracking interval, depends on the nature of organization, and its application area. For this model application, it will be between the 08 am to current time of the same day. Supervisor can select any date and time from the provided GUI date controls, to track or see a mobile unit movement history.

Use Case Name:	Mobile unit tracking.
Actors:	Supervisor.
Trigger:	When ever there is a need of track any mobile unit.
Description:	This use case will happen whenever the supervisor will need to monitor and track a mobile unit, between desired time intervals. Supervisor will select the mobile unit from main application screen and requests to track it, a new screen will open, and by default it display the unit track between 08 am to the current time for the same day. But supervisor could select different time interval and screen will update itself to display intended track of the mobile unit.
Preconditions:	1. Supervisor is logged on to the application. 2. Application Server is running. 3. Connection with the internet is established.
Post conditions:	2. A Map should display in a web browser, which displays track of the mobile unit, along with appropriate date and time GUI controls to see history.
Normal Flow:	1. Supervisor selects the mobile unit from dropdown GUI control provided at main screen. 2. Supervisor pushes the "Track" button on main screen. 3. Alternative flow 1. 4. Alternative flow 2.
Alternative flows:	1. System will process and display the Track of the mobile unit between 08:00:00 to the current time for the same day. 2. System will process and display the track of the mobile unit between the user-selected intervals.
Exceptions:	3. Web server stopped responding. 4. Google Map API doesn't respond.
Actions for Exceptions:	Prompt error message to the user.
Frequency of Use:	Often.
Assumptions:	System works in ideal conditions.
Notes and Issues:	System has implemented in laboratory environment, to observe the limitations. Task is implemented as working prototype with basic

features.

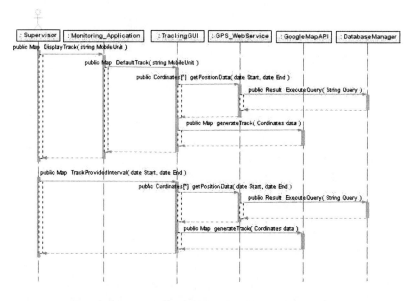

Figure 38: Mobile unit tracking (Sequence Diagram).

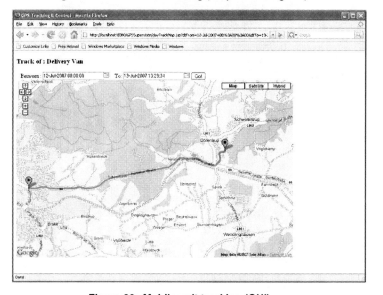

Figure 39: Mobile unit tracking (GUI).

4.5.7 Reporting (Disconnection Period / Messages Status)

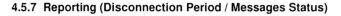
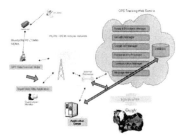

The design objective of this part of the model application is to demonstrate the possible management's reports of the supervisor's interest. Only two reports have discussed and implemented. Kind of reports required for the system are always depends on the requirements of certain applications.

Disconnection Period

This report demonstrates the disconnection time of a mobile unit. The disconnection time means, the time interval for which no positional updates exist for a mobile unit. There could be many reasons, including (hardware & software problems, hazard climate , possible accident, GPS disconnection, and intentional disconnection etc.).

Disconnection Query:- The disconnection period has calculated by comparing the time stamp of each positional update with the next coming update, if the time difference is more then defined tolerance interval (which is 10 minutes in model application) then, that specific record will be included into report data set. The report data set will be displayed in tabular form as showed in figures 40, 43.

Figure 40: Disconnection period query and result.

Use Case Name:	Producing Reports.
Actors:	Supervisor.
Trigger:	When ever there is a need of any specific report.
Description:	This use case will happen whenever supervisor needs special reports about the messages or the disconnection period for a mobile unit, for desired time intervals. Supervisor will select report type and mobile unit from main application screen. He will requests to generate the report. System will open a new screen and by default it display the report containing data between 08 am to the current time for the same day. The supervisor can select different time intervals, and screen will be update it self to display report for intended period.
Preconditions:	1. Supervisor is logged on to the application. 2. Application Server is running. 3. Connection with the internet is established.
Post conditions:	1. A report should be displayed in a web browser, which displays

	intended reports, along with appropriate date and time controls to see records of history.
Normal Flow:	1. Supervisor selects the mobile unit from dropdown control provided at main screen. 2. Supervisor selects the report type from dropdown control provided main screen. 3. Supervisor pushes the "Go" button beside the report type dropdown on main screen. 4. Alternative flow 1. 5. Alternative flow 2.
Alternative flows:	1. System will process and display the default report between 08:00:00 to the current time for the same day. 2. System will process and display the report between the user-selected intervals.
Exceptions:	1. Web server stopped responding. 2. Google Map API doesn't respond.
Actions for Exceptions:	Prompt error message to the user.
Frequency of Use:	Occasionally.
Assumptions:	System works in ideal conditions.
Notes and Issues:	System has implemented in laboratory environment, to observe the limitations. Task is implemented as working prototype with basic reports.

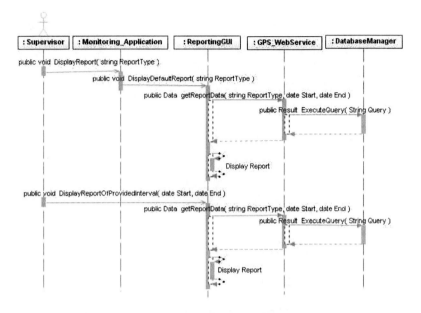

Figure 41: Producing reports (Sequence Diagram).

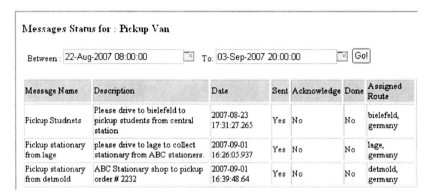

Figure 42: Messages status report.

Disconnection Status for : Pickup Van

Between : 06-Aug-2007 08:00:00   To: 06-Aug-2007 20:00:00   Go!

Disconnected At	Disconnected Untill	Disconnection Period in minutes
2007-08-06 17:06:39.437	2007-08-06 17:17:51.265	11
2007-08-06 17:38:13.906	2007-08-06 17:57:01.843	19
2007-08-06 18:28:39.406	2007-08-06 18:40:28.953	12

Figure 43: Disconnection period report.

4.5.8 System Setup & Configuration

In order to have the model application works properly, there are some configurations required. For the mobile application part of system, the Bluetooth address for the specific GPS device and the position update interval should be configured first time. The monitoring application allow to configure mobile units and system users. If required then the application is able to reset or change configurations. The coming figures illustrates system setup options for proposed simple model application.

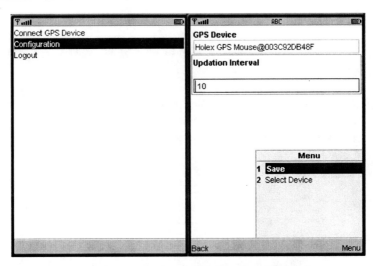

Figure 44: System setup for application on mobile device.

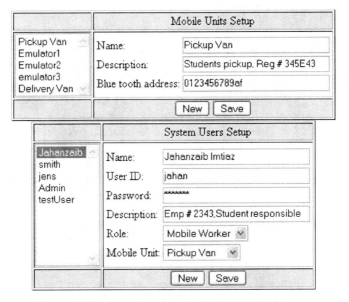

Figure 45: System setup for monitoring application.

4.5.9 Security

This aspect of the proposed application shows, how the security implemented into the system (See Chapter 3).

Intensive security implementation is not in the scope of this study work. The simple security mechanism is adopted by making use of simple security tokens (See Chapter 3) ("*UserID_SessionStartTimestamp_RandomNumber*") based verification. Each token is created when session for particular user starts, and verified on each service request made by the user.

This aspect is divided into two tasks,

- Mobile unit authentication
- Monitoring supervisor authentication

Use Case Name:	Mobile unit authentication.
Actors:	Mobile worker.
Trigger:	When ever mobile worker start application on mobile device.
Description:	This use case will happen when ever mobile worker start application on mobile device. He/she has to login to the system. At first the login procedure asks for user id and password, then it will pass this information together with Bluetooth address of mobile device to the Web Service, that will authenticate the information. If the user is registered and attached with a particular mobile unit then a security token will be generated and sent to mobile unit. A session would be started for the particular user. Each time mobile unit request for a service, that security token will be verified, before granting the access to the service. The session will be closed after logout request and security token will be set to invalid.
Preconditions:	1. The mobile unit, and the user with a role of mobile worker registered into the system and associated together. 2. GPRS is connected.
Post conditions:	1. The user is login to application and a security token should have generated for mobile unit.
Normal Flow:	1. Mobile worker starts the application on mobile device. 2. System shows a screen, that asks user id and password. 3. Mobile worker type information and press login button.

	4. System connects with Web Service to verify registered Bluetooth device and provided user data. 5. Alternative flow 1. 6. Alternative flow 2.
Alternative flows:	1. In case of invalid login data, move to normal flow step 2. 2. In case of valid data, Web Service generate security token and send it to the mobile unit, which will then allow the user to access application.
Exceptions:	3. Web server stopped responding. 4. GPRS connection break.
Actions for Exceptions:	Prompt error message to the user.
Frequency of Use:	Always.
Assumptions:	System works in ideal conditions.
Notes and Issues:	System is implemented in laboratory environment, to observe limitations. Task is implemented as working prototype with basic features.

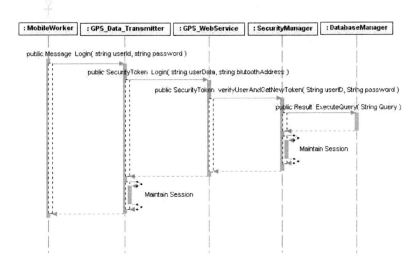

Figure 46: Mobile unit authentication (Sequence Diagram).

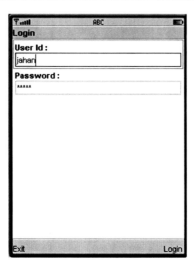

Figure 47: Mobile unit authentication (GUI).

Use Case Name:	Supervisor authentication.
Actors:	Supervisor.
Trigger:	When ever supervisor start monitoring application in browser.
Description:	This use case will happen when ever supervisor try to login into Monitoring & Control application, a login screen would be displayed, that asks user id and password. The provided information will be passed to Web Service for verification. If user registered with supervisor role then a security token will be generated and a session would have started for the particular user. When ever there is a request for any monitoring activity, the security token would be verified before granting the access to the service. The session will be closed after logout request and security token will be set to invalid.
Preconditions:	1. User with role of supervisor exists. 2. Application server is running.
Post conditions:	1. User login to application, a security token generated and session maintained.
Normal Flow:	1. User starts the application in browser.

	2. System asks for user id and password.
	3. User type information and press login button.
	4. System connects with Web Service to verify the provided data.
	5. Alternative flow 1.
	6. Alternative flow 2.
Alternative flows:	1. Invalid login data, move to normal flow step 2.
	2. Valid data, Web Service generate security token and send it to monitoring application to create a session.
Exceptions:	1. Web server stopped responding.
Actions for Exceptions:	Prompt error message to the user.
Frequency of Use:	Always.
Assumptions:	System works in ideal conditions.
Notes and Issues:	System is implemented in laboratory environment. To observer the limitations. Task is implemented as working prototype with basic features.

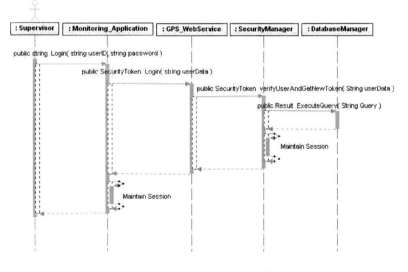

Figure 48: Supervisor authentication (Sequence Diagarm).

Figure 49: Supervisor authentication (GUI).

4.5.10 Data Modeling

The data model is entirely depends on nature of application. The model application is mean to be very simple, so only the most important entities which are essential to realize the Tracking & Control system has used.

In the study work, required data structure is physically implemented in a Java based database management system (See Appendix B). In addition to defining and organizing the data, proposed model also impose (implicitly or explicitly) constraints over the data placed within the structure, as illustrated following figure,

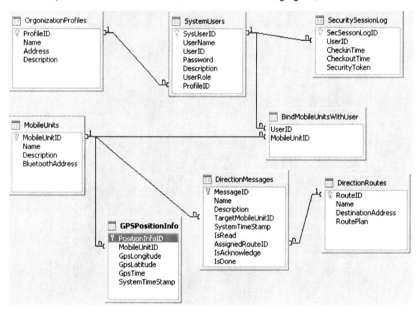

Figure 50: Data modeling

Organizationprofiles:- This table will keep the basic information about organization (an entity interested to track and control its mobile business units).

SystemUsers:- This table will keep the basic information about the system users. The each user will belong to the certain organization. There will be three basic user roles used in model application given as,

- Mobile Worker
- Supervisor
- Admin (create profiles, Web Service maintenance)

SecuritySessionLog:- This table will keep the session and security related information, it also store the unique token for each connected user during a session.

MobileUnits:- This table will keep the information about registered mobile devices.

BindMobileUnitsWithUsers:- This table will associate each mobile device with its operator.

GPSPositionInfo:- This table will keep the actual location information, its temporal changes, and it will keep regular positional updates of each mobile unit.

DirectedMessages:- This table will keep the messages for the mobile worker.

DirectionRoutes:- This table will keep the directional information in textual form, like destination address and route plan from current position to destination.

4.6   Summary

This chapter has presented a detail architecture & design of the model application. Also it have discussed many other architectural possibilities and their draw backs. It also provides an optimum level of design detail to the programmers about different components of the model application.

5   System Test Cases

5.1   Overview

System testing is an integral part of the software development to ensure that application matches with the specification and producing acceptable results. Its also important to identify the flaws of the system to properly intimate to the user. Test cases have broad spectrum, from ensuring the compliance with model architecture, to identify the system bottlenecks and its performance intensive areas.

This study work carries out the some important test cases to see the possible error conditions and to produce appropriate error messages in order to have a stable system, and to identify the cost leakage areas. There are many kinds of possible tests, only the integral ones have been used to demonstrate the credibility of the model application (steps are not mentioned to avoid unnecessary detail) are listed bellow, a list of error messages could be found in Appendix A.

5.2   Forced-Error Tests

They provide or refer to a list of all error conditions and messages. This section identifies the tests that will run to force the application into error conditions.

- *Test case code*:- FET-001
  - o *Description*:- Turn off the Bluetooth device and observe system behavior.
  - o *Application module*:- Mobile application midlet.
  - o *Expected response*:- Display error message 0001.
  - o *Impact on the system*:- There will be no valid position updates which could doubt the system integrity; supervisor will not be able any more to see current location of specific unit. System should maintain a track of disconnected period.
- *Test case code*:- FET-002
  - o *Description*:- GPS coverage stopped, due to some underground tunnel area.
  - o *Application module*:- Mobile application midlet.
  - o *Expected response*:- Display error message 0001.

- o   *Impact on the system:-* There will be no valid position updates which could doubt the system integrity; supervisor will not be able any more to see current location of specific unit, there should be a track of disconnected period, either locally on the mobile device or remotely on the track server.

- *Test case code:-* FET-003

  - o   *Description:-* GPRS connection shut down/ WLAN switch off.

  - o   *Application module:-* Mobile application midlet.

  - o   *Expected response:-* Display error message 0002.

  - o   *Impact on the system:-* Mobile unit will not be operational any more for tracking and control.

- *Test case code:-* FET-004

  - o   *Description:-* Web server shut down.

  - o   *Application module:-* Mobile application midlet.

  - o   *Expected response:-* Display error message 0003.

  - o   *Impact on the system:-* Mobile unit will not be operational for tracking and control.

- *Test case code:-* FET-005

  - o   *Description:-* Mobile device turn off.

  - o   *Application module:-* Monitoring application, mobile application midlet.

  - o   *Expected response:-* Mobile unit will not be operational any more for tracking and control, mobile worker has to restart the device and application.

  - o   *Impact on the system:-* Erroneous shout down would be traceable by session data in security log table. Supervisor will not be able to send the new messages. Supervisor should be able to see disconnected period.

- *Test case code:-* FET-006

  - o   *Description:-* Google Map API turn off.

  - o   *Application module:-* Monitoring application, mobile application midlet.

  - o   *Expected response:-* Display error message 0004.

  - o   *Impact on the system:-* Supervisor will not be able any more to monitor and track the mobile units, mobile worker will not be able to see textual route information.

- *Test case code:-* FET-007

- o *Description*:- Yahoo Map API turn off.

- o *Application module*:- Mobile application midlet.

- o *Expected response*:- Display error message 0005.

- o *Impact on the system*:- Mobile worker will not be able to see Map of the destination.

5.3   Real World User-Level Test

In contrast of forced error tests to find defects, This section identifies the tests that will demonstrate the successful functionalities of the program as expected by its actor. What type of workflow tests should be run? What type of "real work" should be carried out using the application?

- • *Test case code*:- ULT-001

  - o *Description*:- GPS Bluetooth device discovery and communication test.

  - o *Application module*:- Mobile application midlet.

  - o *Expected response*:- User will see the list of available Bluetooth devices and be able to connect with one of them, or he will see the error message 0006.

- • *Test case code*:- ULT-002

  - o *Description*:- Mobile application is able to parse NEMA data, extract correct positional information, and update it on server.

  - o *Application module*:- Mobile application midlet.

  - o *Expected response*:- Supervisor should see the regular positional update from the mobile device, and could be able to track the unit.

- • *Test case code*:- ULT-003

  - o *Description*:- Unit tracking working.

  - o *Application module*:- Monitoring application.

  - o *Expected response*:- Supervisor should be able to see the connected track of specified mobile unit on the Map, or he will see the error message 0008.

- • *Test case code*:- ULT-004

  - o *Description*:- Map display all mobile units in a field.

  - o *Application module*:- Monitoring application.

- o *Expected response:*- Supervisor should be able to see all the mobile units on the main screen of control panel, or will see the error message 0004.

- • *Test case code:*- ULT-005

  - o *Description:*- Verify message sending and receiving.

  - o *Application module:*- Monitoring application, Mobile Application.

  - o *Expected response:*- Supervisor should be able to send a message to the mobile unit, mobile worker should be able to see the upcoming message and its contents, or there should be a known error message from customized list of error messages in Appendix A.

- • *Test case code:*- ULT-006

  - o *Description:*- Mobile user is able to download textual route plan.

  - o *Application module:*- Mobile Application.

  - o *Expected response:*- Mobile worker should be able to request textual route information, system should download the detail route plan for associated destination address and display, or there should an error message 0010.

- • *Test case code:*- ULT-007

  - o *Description:*- Mobile user is able to download a Map of destination.

  - o *Application module:*- Mobile Application.

  - o *Expected response:*- Mobile worker should be able to request destination Map, system should download the Map for associated destination address and display, or there should be an error message 0005.

- • *Test case code:*- ULT-008

  - o *Description:*- Security login authentication.

  - o *Application module:*- Mobile application, Monitoring application.

  - o *Expected response:*- User will logon to the system or he will see the error message 0009.

5.4   **Integration-Level Tests**

This section Identify the components or modules that could be combined and tested independently. This reduces the dependence on the system testing. Identifies any test harnesses or drivers that are need to be developed.

- *Test case code:*- ILT-001

  o *Tag:*- Deploy & test Web Service.

  o *Description:*- Web Service is the core business unit for whole application, if it's up and running properly, its mean system behavior is predictable (See Appendix B).

- *Test case code:*- ILT-002

  o *Tag:*- Deploy & test mobile application.

  o *Description:*- Mobile application is the tier that updates positional information about mobile unit, testing includes Bluetooth connection with GPS device, regular update of data and message receiving mechanism of the application. In case of failure (See Appendix B).

- *Test case code:*- ILT-003

  o *Tag:*- Deploy & test monitoring application.

  o *Description:*- Monitoring application is the tier that facilitates to monitor and control units by means of visually watching them on the Map, and sending them messages, its functionalities should be verified with valid database to make sure it's running properly! In case of failure (See Appendix B).

5.5   System-Level Tests

This section specifies test that will be carried out to fully exercise the application as a whole to ensure that all elements of the integrated system are functioning properly. Note that when a unit and integration testing have been properly performed, the dependence upon system testing can be reduced.

- *Test case code:*- SLT-001

  o *Tag:*- Tracking & control system operation in lab environment using WLAN, deployment of the system with all components.

  o *Description:*- Objective of this test is to verify the whole system in a lab environment using WLAN, to identify the components of malfunction, to exercise fixes and to make sure that model application is complied with the requirements to run smoothly.

- *Test case code:*- SLT-002

  o *Tag:*- Tracking & control system operation in open field using GPRS, deployment of the system with all components.

o *Description*:- Objective of this test is to verify the whole system in a real world environment, to see how system behaves when actually deployed on the physical tiers using GPRS data communication. It observes the system latency, potential risk of failure, cost of operations, in order to identifying influential factors.

5.6   Summary

Testing a software application is always an integral part of the software development process. This section has discussed the vital scenarios that should and have been tested to ensure compliance of physical application with the design specification   as   discussed   in   chapter   4.

6   Conclusion and Future Work

6.1   Conclusion

This study has presented a novel approach, by means of a cost effective and portable Route Transmission & Control Web Service, a GPS location transmitter mobile Web Service client and a monitoring web application. It has provided a foundation for construction of cost effective LTCS using SOAP messages based on client/server model. The achievements of the project are described below.

- This study argues that utilizing the GPRS and Web Services are better methods to achieve cost efficient data exchange as compare to traditional approaches (SMS, WAP push, GSM dialup networks). It demonstrates this by describing previous and traditional approaches, followed by a comparative analysis of these technologies in the context of *Eben-Ezer* specific scenarios of positional data exchange.

- The theoretical idea presented in this study work has been applied to real-world LTCS application (for *Eben-Ezer* that manages relatively small number of vehicles). A reference software implementation is presented, which illustrates the phenomena of interoperability, by demonstrating the ability to allow a party to play a role of the monitoring authority. By means of *SupervisorWebApplication* to, register, monitor and direct fleet of mobile units. Which is done in form of instructional messages and textual routes (Also demonstrated possibility of sending directional Map of destinations).

- The proposed Web Service is based on an open source Java EE5 technology. That makes it portable and gives advantage over the software development cost. It is also very simple in design and GUI, which gives the advantages on existing applications, because it requires less time of deployment in operational environment and to train the application users (*Eben-Ezer*).

- The use of a GPRS for data communication in model application, improves the response time, makes it less probable to lose the track of mobile object as compaired to traditional SMS based applications.

- The proposed application allows variable location update intervals (because of cost advantage). Shorter interval allows to have a more dense positional data in the urban areas (small roads, less distances, many streets) to provide sharp traces, which could not be possible using SMS based systems because of cost and unpredictable message delivery time. Where as a greater update interval reduces the amount of data on the track server (which improves query response time), and it will not impact the quality of the visual track history on Map, because in countryside vehicles are normally drive on long highways.

- More importantly, the proposed application has demonstrated, the efficient, existing and future, SOAP messages solution techniques to be effectively applied to solving extensibility problems. For example the same model application can be adopted to provide wide range of services to the diverse classes of consumers and have implications for LTCS's as a whole.

- Furthermore, this study work has also provided the guidelines to the cost efficient application design strategies to achieve maximum information through minimum data transfer.

6.2   Problems Faced & Suggestions

There are certainly some problems faced during the course of study work, including some technical programming related issues in some parts of application, and some design related problems. Those need to be addressed in future, during development of full fledge opera   tional system. Some of them are described as following,

- At this stage the address of WSDL URL was hardcoded into the mobile Web Service client (because of Netbean's implementation), it creates stubs that based on WSDL file so its not possible to dynamically determine the Web Service at run time.

- Some configuration issues like, incorporating logical address in WSDL Soap address section still need to be addressed, to deploy and test proposed Web Service in a real world environment.

- To generate the textual direction, a third party component *WebRenderer* has been used which is platform dependent. More work needs to be done to replace this third party component, by providing a mechanism to parse and execute the JavaScript API provided by Google MAP Service.

- The disconnection report query needs to be further optimized in order to cope with the location database of larger magnitude.

- The model application generates some basic reports for a proof of concept, further work will be required for improvement and enhancements.

- Although the developed model application is a quite stable. But the project is developed under Netbeans 6.0 IDE which is itself in evolution stages, there were some compatibility issues encountered during the course of project.

- Mobile phones are used to test and debug the application, which doesn't support Java Location API 179, so the application required extra coding to handle the formatting issues of location data received from Bluetooth GPS mouse.

- LTCS operational cost estimates are tentative, calculation based on individual service provider companies. Mostly vary from country to country (Calculated for Germany) involving many factors, including network service provider (O2 in our case) charges, type of hardware used, and profit margins etc.

6.3   Future Work

There are some practical and theoretical issues that need to be addressed, however. On the practical side, there is a need to use some SOAP envelop compression techniques to further reduce the data size [28]. There is a need to look into wireless web-service architecture, based on the smart client model that can address some of the fundamental differences between the Wireless and Wiredline Environments [53]-54], and QoS issues for Web Services in Mobile Environment [28]. More work is required in the area of securing Web Service in a mobile environment. Need to work on integration of the ability to register, discover, and govern Web Service as a part of SOA. Currently system has demonstrated the successful download and display of destination Map on mobile device, but more work require to incorporate traces of driving direction on the Map for more visualization and better guidance.

On the theoretical side, the analysis of the complexity of the present approach is rather informal. Much remains to be done in this regard, especially when comparing to the complexity of existing applications. For this comparison, additional work will be required to adapt the current Functional & Architectural design to suit existing applications and more real time problems. Optimization of stored location information, and Web Service response time for client queries over the data of such magnitude, is an important area that requires further work.

While working on this study the intension was to provide a common frame work for development of cost effective Web Service that supports Route Transmission & Control for small scale applications. And at the same time it should be a platform independent and interoperable with many other applications. This work hopes to be a first step towards further understanding this important issue.

References

[1] Safefreight Technology Ltd. Alberta, Canada (http://www.safefreight.com) [visited April 2007].

[2] Comprehensive Contractual Descriptions of Web Services by Vladimir Tosic & Bernard Pagurek , University of Western Ontario, Canada, vladat@computer.orgOn [2005].

[3] GALILEO, European Satellite Navigation System. (http://ec.europa.eu/dgs /energy_transport /galileo/ applications/road_fr.htm) [visited April 2007].

[4] Global Tracking Communications Inc. (http://www.gpstrackit.com/?trackcode=bizcom) [Last visited April 2007].

[5] ThinkGeo Inc. (http://thinkgeo.com/) [visited April 2007].

[6] Wikipedia: web encyclopedia "General packet radio service [GPRS], SMS, WAP push, The spiral model, Telematics, SOAP, Vehicle tracking system, Global positioning system ", (http://en.wikipedia.org/wiki/) [visited Spetember 2007].

[7] WAP Based Location Services , Slim Souissi and Garland Phillips [Motorola], (http://www.w3.org/ Mobile/ posdep/MotorolaW3C.html) [visited May 2007].

[8] IDC Communications Inc. (http://www.idccommunications.com/corporate /loadtrak_cellular _tracking .asp) [visited May 2007].

[9] Spook Tech. (http://www.spooktech.com/trackingeqmt/index.shtml) [visited June 2007].

[10] Privacy Spot, "Data privacy forum" (http://www.privacyspot.com/?q=node/view/774) [visited June 2007].

[11] DeveryWare S.A. Paris France, "GSM vs. GPS", (http://www.deveryware.com/article.php3 ?id_article=26) [visited June 2007].

[12] Pegasus Technologies Inc, "RF Tracking vs. GPS Tracking" (http://www.pegtech.com /rfgps.htm) [visited June 2007].

[13] Pegasus Technologies Inc, "Stolen Vehicle Recovery System" (http://www.vectortrac.com/) [visited June 2007].

[14] LoJack Corporation, "Stollen Vehilce Recovery System" (http://www.lojack.com/) [visited July 2007].

[15] Internodal International, "SNAPPI RF™ Automotive " (http://www.internodalinternational.com /prdrfaut .htm) [visited July 2007].

[16] NEC Corporation, "RAN architecture using RS/RRH", (http://www.nec-mobilesolutions.com/ infrastructures/solution/distributed_nb.html) [visited July 2007].

[17] GPS Tracking NZ Ltd, (http://www.gpstracking.co.nz/) [Last visited August 2007].

[18] Aspicore Ltd, "Aspicore GSM Tracker" (http://www.aspicore.com/en/tuotteet_tracker_ diagram.asp ? tab=2&sub=2) [visited August 2007].

[19] Global Tracking Communications Inc,"GPS Tracking - FAQ" (http://www.gpstrackit.com /faq.html) [visited August 2007].

[20] ITERIS ,"National ITS Architecture" (http://www.iteris.com/itsarch/html/entity/paents.htm) [visited August 2007].

[21] U.S. Department of Transportation's ,"Intelligent transportation systems (ITS)" (http://www.
      its.dot.gov/ its_overview.htm) [visited August 2007].

[22] The USDOT ITS Standards Program ,"Intelligent transportation systems (ITS)" (http://www.
      standards.its.dot.gov/default.asp) [visited August 2007].

[23] IEEE Vehicular Technology Society ,"Connecting the Mobile World" (http://vtsociety.org/)
      [visited Spetember 2007].

[24] NEMA, GPSInformation.Net ,"Forums for standardization of electrical equipment, and GPS
      data formats" (http://www.nema.org/about/, http://www.gpsinformation.org/dale/nmea.htm)
      [visited Spetember 2007].

[25] STARFISH Positioning Solutions, "A GPRS based Automatic Vehicle Locator vs. SMS based
      Automatic Vehicle Locator", (http://www.my-starfish.com/brochure/STARFISH_GPRS_ VS_
      SMS.pdf) [visited Spetember 2007].

[26] SearchWrap.com "Online community for IT specialists, [Try GPRS SMS texting to reduce the
      cost of sending international SMS abroad]", (http://searchwarp.com/swa216908.htm) [visited
      Spetember 2007].

[27] HHFR: A new architecture for Mobile Web Services Principles and Implementations
      by Sangyoon Oh and Geoffrey C. Fox Community Grids Laboratory 501 N Morton St. 222,
      Bloomington, IN, 47408, USA. gcf}@indiana.edu [2004].

[28] Measuring Availability of Mobile Web Services by Kee-Leong Tan, S.M.F.D. Syed Mustapha
      Asian Research Centre, British Telecommunications Group, Cyberview Lodge Office
      Complex, Hibiscus Block, 1st Floor, 63000 Cyberjaya, Selangor Darul Ehsan, Malaysia [2005].

[29] Microsoft "MapPoint Web Service", http://www.microsoft.com/mappoint/products/webservice/
      default.mspx) [visited June 2007].

[30] Yahoo! Maps Web Services Map Image API, http://developer.yahoo.com/maps/rest/V1
      /mapImage .html) [Last visited May 2007].

[31] Google! Maps Web Services - Google Map API, (www.google.com/apis/maps/) [visited May
      2007].

[32] ArcWeb Services "Map database", (http://www1.arcwebservices.com/v2006/index.jsp) [visited
      June 2007].

[33] NOKIA Developers Forum "JSR179 Location API for J2ME" (http://www.forum.nokia.com/
      document/Java_ME_Developers_Library_v2/GUID-4AEC8DAF-DDCC-4A30-B820-
      23F2BA60EA52/overview-summary.html) [visited June 2007].

[34] NetBeans Location Based Services Mobility Demo, (http://www.netbeans.org/kb/50/mobility-
      lbs-demo.html) [visited June 2007].

[35] The Saskatchewan Institute of Applied Science and Technology (SIAST) CANADA,
      "Geographic Information Science for Resource Management Woodland Campus",
      (http://www.siast.sk.ca/siast/educationtraining/oncampusprograms/7263/6143/5854/index)
      [visited October 2007].

[36] Tramigo UK,"Secure Mobile Asset Tracking", (http://www.tramigo.co.uk/) [visited October
      2007].

[37] Soniya Technologies USA, "GPS Tracking Services, Device, and Solutions", (http://www.
      soniyatech.com/) [visited October 2007].

[38] Anything GPS, "GPS Vehicle Tracking", (http://www.anythinggps.com/index.asp?PageAction=
      VIEWCATS&Category=5) [visited October 2007].

[39] GPS Fleet Solutions, (http://www.gpsfleetsolutions.com/About_GPS_Fleet_Solutions.php) [visited October 2007].

[40] BRICKHOUSE Security USA,"GPS System Used By Police and Private Investigators", (http://www.brickhousesecurity.com/slimtrak-realtime-gps-tracking-car-locator.html) [visited October 2007].

[41] HunterPro USA, "High Level GPS based Security Solutions", (http://www.hunterpro.com/ GPS/GPS-vehicle-tracking.html) [visited October 2007].

[42] Vision Guard Systems UK,"Live tracking using mobile phone",(http://www.visionguard-anpr.co.uk/html/tracking.html) [visited October 2007].

[43] Burbridge Detective Agency, "Vehicle Tracking - GPS", (http://www.burbridgepi.com/html/ vehicle _tracking_-_gps_.html) [visited October 2007].

[44] Web Services Security: SOAP Message Security 1.1 (WS-Security 2004) OASIS Standard Specification, (http://www.oasis-open.org/committees/download.php/16790/wss-v1.1-spec-os-SOAP MessageSecurity.pdf) [visited October 2007].

[45] The Liberty Alliance by Paul Madsen April 01, 2003 (http://webservices.xml.com/ pub/a/ws /2003/04/01/liberty.html) [visited October 2007].

[46] Liberty Alliance, "Web Service secure interoperability", (http://www.projectliberty.org/) [visited September 2007].

[47] J. Cuellar, Siemens AG, J. Morris Center for Democracy & Technology D. Mulligan, Samuelson Law, Technology & Public Policy Clinic J. Peterson NeuStar, J. Polk Cisco [February 2004].

[48] IBM WebSphere Developer Technical Journal,"Web Services Security ",(http://www.ibm.com/ developerworks/websphere/techjournal/0404_bose/0404_bose.html) [visited Spetember 2007].

[49] Department of Education, Training and Arts Queensland, Australia,"Global positioning system", (http://education.qld.gov.au/curriculum/area/maths/compass/html/satnavsystems/ sawha.html) [visited Septemebr 2007].

[50] The Aerospace Corporation USA, "GPS segments" ,(http://www.aero.org/education/primers /gps/ images/major-segments.jpg) [visited Septemebr 2007].

[51] GPS Personal Locator,(http://www.gpspersonallocator.com/guard/images/gpsglobe.jpg) [visited October 2007].

[52] GPS Store, (http://www.thegpsstore.com/images/gps-systems-satellites-triangulation.jpg) [visited October 2007].

[53] Challenges: Wireless Web Services by Hao-hua Chu, Chuang-wen You, Chao-ming Teng Department of Computer Science and Information Engineering NTU, Taipei, Taiwan (hchu@csie.ntu.edu.tw, r91023@csie.ntu.edu.tw, jt@csie.ntu.edu.tw) [2004].

[54] Wireless SOAP: Optimizations for Mobile Wireless Web Services, by Naresh Apte, Keith Deutsch, Ravi Jain, DoCoMo USA Labs {apte@docomolabs-usa.com, deutsch@docomolabs-usa.com, jain@docomolabs-usa.com} [2005].

[55] Geospatial Web Services: An Evolution of Geospatial Data Infrastructure By Athanasios Tom Kralidis, Department of Geography and Environmental Studies Carleton University [2005]

Appendix A: Error messages

This section provides the list of error messages, that could be encounter during the operation of the model application. Also the appropriate actions are discussed to keep system running predictably.

1. *Error Message Code:*- 0001

   o *Error Messages:*- "Unable to connect with GPS device"

   o *Description:*- This error message appears when the user tries to connect with the pre configured GPS Mouse.

   o *Recommended Action:*- Verify that Bluetooth GPS mouse is switched-on (See Appendix B).

2. *Error Message Code:*- 0002

   o *Error Messages:*- "Connection with GPRG failed"

   o *Description:*- This error message appears when the application tries to connect with the internet to communicate with the Web Service.

   o *Recommended Action:*- Verify registration of the packet data service, verify the correct GPRS configuration from the service provider.

3. *Error Message Code:*- 0003

   o *Error Messages:*- "Tracking Service unavailable"

   o *Description:*- This error message appears when the application tries to communicate with the Web Service.

   o *Recommended Action:*- Verify application server is running (See Appendix B).

4. *Error Message Code:*- 0004

   o *Error Messages:*- "Unable to display Map object"

   o *Description:*- This error message appears when the application tries to display a Map to the supervisor for the monitoring of mobile units.

   o *Recommended Action:*- Verify the browser compatibility, verify the JavaScript option is on, and verify if the correct key is created for accessing Google Map Service.

5. *Error Message Code:*-0005

   o *Error Messages:*- "Unable to download the Map image"

Jahanzaib Imtiaz

- o *Description:-* This error message appears when the mobile application tries to download the Map of destination.

- o *Recommended Action:-* Verify the correct key is created for accessing yahoo Map service, verify the Web Service have enough privileges to write image file on server, verify the directory folder path is appropriate and accessible. The model application do not supports this feature for the detail (a street level) address of destination, verify that the only a main city is mentioned in the destination address, for example "Detmold, Germany".

6. *Error Message Code:-* 0006

   - o *Error Messages:-* "No GPS device found"

   - o *Description:-* This error message appears when the mobile application tries to discover the Bluetooth device with GPS service running on it.

   - o *Recommended Action:-* Verify availability of GPS mouse, and verify if it's switched-on.

7. *Error Message Code:-* 0007

   - o *Error Messages:-* "Unable to send position data"

   - o *Description:-* This error message appears when the mobile application tries to receive positional data from GPS device and send it to the server.

   - o *Recommended Action:-* Try to restart GPS device, also try to relocate it, possible reason could be the malformed NEMA sentence data packets (See Appendix D and Chapter 2).

8. *Error Message Code:-* 0008

   - o *Error Messages:-* ""Data of selected interval not found""

   - o *Description:-* This error message appears when the supervisor tries to produce track of mobile unit, or while generating report that include user provided time intervals.

   - o *Recommended Action:-* Verify time and date values and try again by providing logically valid date & time.

9. *Error Message Code:-* 0009

   - o *Error Messages:-* "Login failed!...verify user data"

   - o *Description:-* This error message appears when the mobile worker or supervisor connects to application server for authentication.

   - o *Recommended Action:-* Verify user data and try again, the user id or password is case sensitive in model application.

10. *Error Message Code:-* 0010

- o *Error Messages:-* "Unable to retrieve textual route"

- o *Description:-* This error message appears when the mobile worker try to retrieve textual route information, which is associated with a message.

- o *Recommended Action:-* Possible reason could be invalid address, Another reason could be malfunction of third party content render component, try to restart the application server.

Appendix B: Development Environment Setup, Installation & Deployment Guidelines

This guide aims to describe and provide the details of, the development environment setup steps for the model application, the installation & deployment steps of the application with all components at all tiers, The configuration steps for the application, and the application startup setup.

The application is deployed and tested on Microsoft Windows XP and MAC OS X 10.4.9 platforms. It uses Symbian OS based on WLAN enabled Sony Ericsson P990i and Nokia E65. The intentions of study work is to develop a platform independent model application, but the used third party WebRenderer component is not platform independent and have separate versions for Mac, Linux and Windows XP. This makes model application not completely platform independent. Excluding the functionalities of that WebRenderer, and introducing some customized alternative (which is not in scope of the study work) could make system perfectly platform independent.

The mobile application part developed on Windows XP, because of its better mobility pack support for Netbean 6.0. But its binary distribution (.jar) proved to be platform independent.

Development Environment Setup

<u>**Required software and hardware resources**</u>

1. Hardware

   - Bluetooth enabled GPS Mouse (Holux GPSlim 236).

   - Bluetooth enabled PDA or Mobile Device (3G) With GPRS / WAP configuration settings.

   - Type of phone used in the lab environment (Sony Ericson 990i, Nikia E65, SE K700i, and Nokia 6280). There could be any other 3G mobile device (PDA) that supports Bluetooth and GPRS functionalities (See Chapter 2).

   - Desktop PC, which has running Windows XP with service pack 2 along with Java supported web application server, and it is exposed to the WWW via unique IP address.

   - Also tested at MAC OS X 10.4.9, memory 1 GB 667 MHz, processor 2GHz.

- Minimum Ram should be 1GB or above, processor should be 1.8 GHz or above.

- DSL based High speed internet connection.

2. Software (source)

- Java supported Integrated Development Environment (NetBeans 6.0 M10, http://www.netbeans.org/).

- JDK1.6.0 (http://java.sun.com/javase/downloads/index.jsp).

- Application server (Sun Java System Application Server 9.0).

- Third party component WebRenderer Swing Edition version 4.0 (http://www.webrenderer.com/products/swing/product/).

- Internet Explorer version 6.0 or greater, Or Mozilla Firefox version 6.0 or greater, All with JavaScript Enabled.

- Project folder GPSTrackerWebservice (attached CD).

- Project folder GPSSupervisor (See Attached CD).

- Project folder GPSTransmitter (See Attached CD).

- Database structure script file (See Attached CD).

- GPSRouteControl database structure folder (See Attached CD).

Steps

This step involve deployment of all the component of application

1. Download and install NetBean 6.0 M10

2. Download WebRenderer 4.0 swing component's evaluation version

3. Run NetBean Integrated development environment

4. Go Tools→ Java DB Database → Create Database

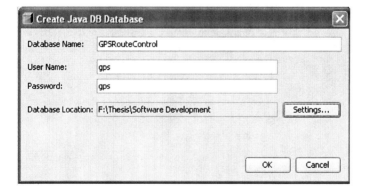

5. Execute provided database script to generate tables into Execute command window opened, by Databases→ JDBC:GPSRouteControl → Tables→ Right Click→Execute Command

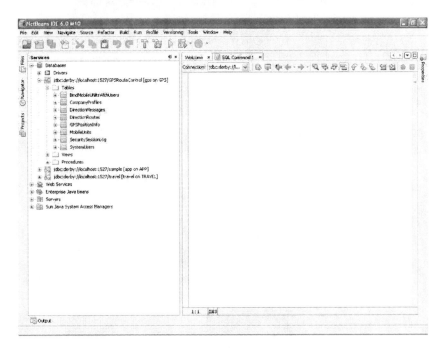

6. Or place "GPSRouteControl" JavaDB structured database folder into default database location

7. You can also change the database location from NetBean Tools→ Java DB Database → Settings→ Database Location

8. Open the services panel and select the databases node and then select the driver connected to newly created database, right click and select connect provide user name and password, press ok. Database should be connected and show data model.

9. Open following projects from the provided attached CD, into NetBeans IDE,

   ▪ GPSTrackerWebservice

   ▪ GPSSupervisor

   ▪ GPSTransmiter

GPSTrackerWebservice

1. Resolve the reference problem by adding WebRenderer component in class library, by right clicking project node→ Properties → Libraries→ Add Jar/ Folder

2. Expend GPSTrackerWebservice project navigate to Web Pages folder and open SystemProperties.xml file, it will have following properties that need to be configured before fully deploy the application.

   - DATABASE_URL= jdbc:{derby/Or used driver name}:// {HostServerNameOrIP}:{AccessPort}/{DatabaseName}
   - DATABASE_DRIVER= org.apache.derby.jdbc.ClientDriver
   - DATABASE_USER={DatabaseUserName}
   - DATABASE_PASSWORD={DatabaseUserPassword}
   - HOST_SERVER_URL=http://HostServerNameOrIP/
   - PROXY_SERVER_IP
   - PROXY_SERVER_PORT
   - YAHOO_API_KEY (Go to yahoo web site (http://developer. yahoo.com/maps/rest/V1/mapImage.html) and generate key after providing the HOST_SERVER_URL)
   - GOOGLEMAP_API_KEY (Go to Google web site (http://www. google.com/apis/maps/signup.html) and generate key after providing the HOST_SERVER_URL)

3. Right click the GPSTrackerWebservice project node and click "undeploy and deploy"

4. Type following URL's in browser, it should display an xml based Web Service description http://HOST_SERVER_URL/GPSTrackerWebservice/GPSRouteMonitor Service?wsdl

GPSSupervisor

1. Right click the GPSSupervisor project node and click New→ Web Service client

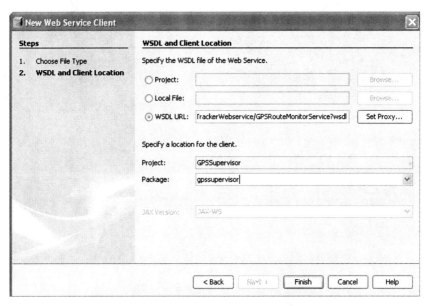

2. Provide the correct WSDL URL and package name, and then press finish. A Web Service reference GPSRouteMonitorService should have been created.

3. Right click the GPSSupervisor project node and click undeploy and deploy.

GPSTransmiter

1. Now to install the mobile application part, first Author has to add the Web Service reference into project, because it require hard coded WSDL address for the mobile Web Service client, which can only be provided after deployment of GPSTrackerWebservice

2. Right click the GPSTransmiter project node and click New→ J2ME Web Service Client

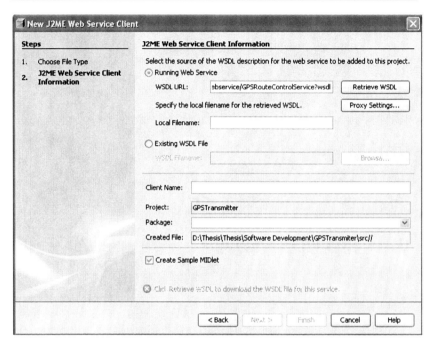

- o Give a suitable package name and click Retrieve WSDL.

- o Stub class and some other resource class would automatically generate.

- o Open GPSRouteControlService_Stub.java replace function java_lang_String_ArrayfromObject with following code (there is a bug in NetBeans 6.0M10. While automatically generating Web Services mobile client, it doesn't make correct conversion of string array data type and always throw exception).

```
private static java.lang.String[] java_lang_String_ArrayfromObject( Object obj[] ) {
    java.lang.String result[] = new java.lang.String[obj.length];
    for( int i = 0; i < obj.length; i++ ) {
        result[i] = new java.lang.String();
        result[i] = (String) obj[i];
    }
    return result;
}
```

3. Right click the GPSTransmiter project node and click clean & build the project.

4. Connect the cable of a particular mobile device with USB port of the computer and install the GPSTransmiter.jar file. The file will be available at distribution folder in project directory.

5. Application setup would be complete and application should be ready for its first go!

The application deployment using binary distribution packages is also possible. The administrator of Java Application Server may install GPSTrackerWebservice and GPSSupervisor monitoring application, by using their .war distribution files. But the mobile GPS data transmitter application need to recompile any way, because it take the hardcoded WSDL URL to create mobile Web Service client. That's why it's better to deploy application using development environment, it will provide a better control on configuration issues.

Application startup setup

- Open GPSSupervisor web application, register a new mobile unit and attach it to a user having mobile worker role.

- Start the GPSTracker application from the mobile device.

- Login to the server with specific user id and password.

- Go to the configuration menu and set the GPS device and the update interval.

Jahanzaib Imtiaz

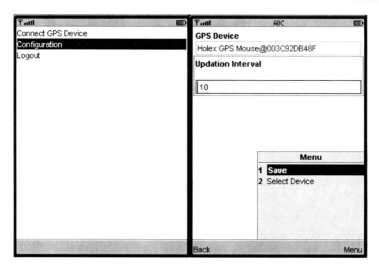

- Connect with the GPS device; Web Service should start receiving positional updates.

Appendix C: GPRG Configuration

This section would describe the GPRS connection setting for mobile device.

Steps

1. Request for GPRS/WAP settings from provider, by calling them or from their web side, following link can also be used
   https://nokiags.wdsglobal.com/advanced?siteLanguageId=118

2. Save the configuration came by SMS.

3. Set them active

4. Browse any web site from mobile device (mail.yahoo.com)

5. If internet connection working

6. Run the ConnectionTest midlet application

7. Press connect option from menu

8. It will ask for network connection access

9. Accept and allow the network connection

10. Wait for few movements, screen should display an XML file from source (http://www.w3schools.com/xml/note.xml)

11. If above steps work fine, then mobile application should work at that mobile phone.

Appendix D: NEMA (GGA)

$GPGGA,123519,4807.038,N,01131.000,E,1,08,0.9,545.4,M,46.9,M,,*47

Where:

GGA   Global Positioning System Fix Data

123519   Fix taken at 12:35:19 UTC

4807.038,N   Latitude 48 deg 07.038' N

01131.000,E   Longitude 11 deg 31.000' E

1   Fix quality: 0 = invalid

                1 = GPS fix (SPS)

                2 = DGPS fix

                3 = PPS fix

        4 = Real Time Kinematic

        5 = Float RTK

                6 = estimated (dead reckoning) (2.3 feature)

        7 = Manual input mode

        8 = Simulation mode

08   Number of satellites being tracked

0.9   Horizontal dilution of position

545.4,M   Altitude, Meters, above mean sea level

46.9,M   Height of geoid (mean sea level) above WGS84 ellipsoid

(empty field) time in seconds since last DGPS update

(empty field) DGPS station ID number

*47   the checksum data, always begins with *

Printed in the United States
122400LV00004B/50/P

9 783836 475068